THE GREAT
BBQ SAUCE
BOOK

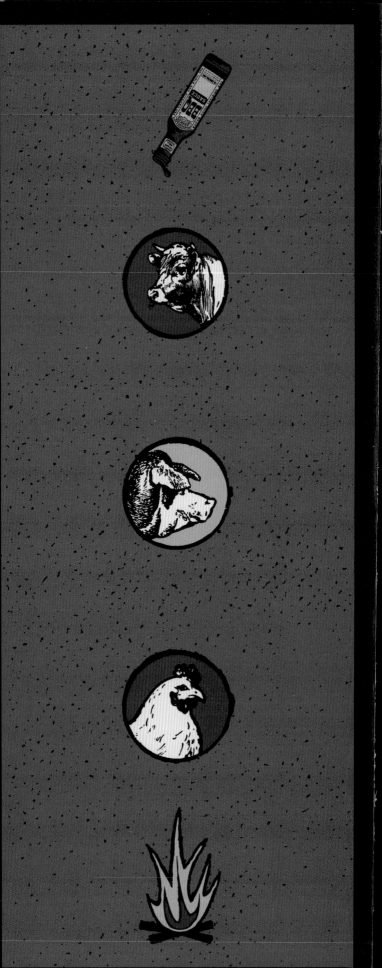

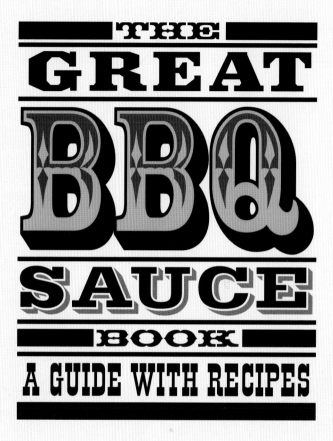

THE GREAT BBQ SAUCE BOOK

A GUIDE WITH RECIPES

BY ARDIE A. DAVIS

TEN SPEED PRESS
BERKELEY, CALIFORNIA

FOR GEORGIA BUCHANAN, AWARD-WINNING KANSAS CITY ENTREPRENEUR
AND HONORARY CHAIR, AMERICAN ROYAL INTERNATIONAL BARBECUE
SAUCE, RUB & BASTE CONTEST.

IN MEMORY OF JUNIOUS "BUCK" BUCHANAN, DEFENSIVE LINEMAN, KANSAS
CITY CHIEFS; PRO FOOTBALL HALL OF FAME INDUCTEE; HONORARY
CHAIR, AMERICAN ROYAL INTERNATIONAL BARBECUE SAUCE CONTEST,
UNTIL HIS DEATH IN 1992.

Copyright © 1999 by Ardie A. Davis

Ten Speed Press
P.O. Box 7123
Berkeley, CA 94707
www.tenspeed.com

Distributed in Australia by Simon and Schuster Australia, in
Canada by Ten Speed Press Canada, in New Zealand by Southern
Publishers Group, in South Africa by Real Books, and in the
United Kingdom and Europe by Airlift Books.

Cover design by Design Site
Interior design by Paul Kepple
Photography by Jonathan Chester/Extreme Images

Library of Congress Cataloging-in-Publication Data

Davis, Ardie.
The great BBQ sauce book : a guide with recipes.
p. cm.
includes bibliographical references and index.
ISBN 0-89815-944-X (alk. paper)
1. Barbecue cookery. 2. Barbecue sauce. I. Title.
TX840.B3P69 1999
641.5'784—dc2198-42434
CIP

First printing, 1999
Printed in China.

2 3 4 5 6 7 8 9 10—03 02 01 00 99

CONTENTS

CONTINUED

GLOSSARY - 146

SOURCES - 149

INDEX - 157

It's DELICIOUS

ACKNOWLEDGMENTS

Not long ago, Dennis Hayes called me unexpectedly from California and asked me to do this book. It didn't take long to say yes. Throughout the process, from idea to reality, Dennis has been a delight to work with. He loves food and people and the publishing industry.

After signing the contract, the magnitude of the task felt, at times, overwhelming. Fortunately, at the beginning of the project, I was reading Anne Lamott's book about writing, *Bird by Bird*. She tells a story about her younger brother. Facing a next-day deadline for a term paper project about birds that he had had three months to write, he was feeling totally overwhelmed. His father wisely advised him to proceed "bird by bird." Thank you, Anne, for helping me focus, sauce by sauce.

Over the past several years I have gained a lot of firsthand experience with barbecue sauces as founder and tastemaster of the American Royal International Barbecue Sauce, Rub & Baste Contest. Several loyal committee members have been extremely helpful and inspirational to me. Bill McVay, who agreed to chair the event, has done innovative wonders with his leadership skills. Steve and Janice Katz have managed the Diddy-Wa-Diddy Barbecue Store from the few bottles Steve sold on a whim to passersby after the fourth contest. Paul Kirk has taught me a lot about the anatomy of sauces and has served as head pitmaster since the second year. He was a judge the first year and decided I could use some help cooking. Johnny White, Karen Putnam, Dan Morey, and Fast Eddy Maurin serve admirably as associate pitmasters. Brian Heinecke applies his management and marketing skills to the complicated logistics of the contest. Bill and Becky Collison do setup and troubleshooting. Heather Bowman and team, of Pricewaterhouse Coopers, tallies the ballots. If space permitted, I would thank more than a hundred other loyal volunteers by name.

In addition to Dennis Hayes, the editors at Ten Speed have been a pleasure to work with. I value their upbeat attitude, their competence, and their professionalism. Special thanks to Jason Rath for bringing this book to the finish.

My wife, Gretchen, was a tremendous help in sharing her opinions of some of the sauces. She had no small task, tolerating the hundreds of bottles of sauce throughout the house and the disruption of our life together while this book was in process. Thanks to my daughter and my son-in-law, Sarah and Alan, for discovering some of the sauces in this book. Thanks to Lee, my son, for comments on some of the sauces, and for encouragement.

Finally, my thanks and respect to the people who make, distribute, and sell barbecue sauces.

INTRODUCTION

WELCOME TO A SPICY ADVENTURE. *The Great BBQ Sauce Book* will serve you as a primer, source listing, and user's guide to a booming industry where everybody believes that his or her sauce is the best in the world.

In one handy, portable volume, you get:
· A user's guide to what sauces can and cannot do for you
· Tasting notes on over 300 commercially available sauces
· Glimpses of some colorful people who make barbecue their passion and their life
· Source information on where to get enough sauce to keep your cupboards stocked for a lifetime and beyond (yes, a recommended "burial sauce" is included)
· A glossary of some words that are essential to understanding barbecue
· Tips on books and home pages for learning more about sauce
· Some creative recipes for putting your sauces to work

SWEET, TANGY, AND FIERY

At one time, different regions featured only one style of barbecue sauce. Thanks to migration and an escalating appetite for culinary diversity, it is now possible to enjoy a variety of barbecue sauces wherever you live.

Although generalizations can be made about typical sauces in various regions, sauces that are exceptions to the local rule are easy to find. Consumers today demand more choices. Yet, in the United States, most barbecue sauces are tomato-based. Exceptions to tomato bases in parts of the South are mustard, vinegar, and white sauce. In the Southwest you'll find a full spectrum of sauces from sweet to tangy, mild to fiery, and in parts of Texas, no sauce at all, except maybe some red pepper sauce or a jalapeño pepper on the side. Fruit-based sauces and fruits in other sauce bases are becoming increasingly popular in the United States. Other countries, such as the Philippines and various Latin American countries, have put fruit to good use as a barbecue condiment for many years.

Although you'll find references to "Memphis-style" or "Southwestern accent" or "Texas tanginess" in this book, I chose not to organize sauces by region. Since the focus is on barbecue sauce flavors, I decided to present these sauces under three broad flavor categories: sweet, tangy, and fiery.

Even those distinctions have some limitations. Some sauces are close to equal in sweetness or tanginess. Some sauces that are mild to me may be fiery to you, or vice versa. The judgment calls are mine.

If your palate doesn't agree with mine on a particular sauce, there is room on each page to make your own notes. I encourage you to do this. In fact, Richard W. Clements, author of *The Book in America* and associate librarian at the Kansas University Kenneth Spencer Research Library, says that the historical value of a book is increased immensely when personalized with handwritten notes. Be advised, however, that used book dealers will decrease the value of a personalized book, unless it bears the marks of a famous person. Although I land on the Clements side of the issue, the choice is yours.

BARBECUE SAUCE USER'S GUIDE

Here's what you need to get the best and most out of barbecue sauce:

- An open mind. Be open to trying sauces that stretch your concepts of how a barbecue sauce should taste.
- Flexibility. Many barbecue sauces will complement more foods than barbecue meat. Be flexible enough to experiment and try new combinations of food and sauce.
- Proper tools and equipment. Proper equipment includes a stainless steel saucepan for stovetop sauce heating, ceramic bowls and ramekins for oven or microwave heating and for sauce/food presentation, wooden spoons for stirring, ceramic spoons for tasting, disposable plastic squeeze bottles for sauce painting, and a good shower or nearby car wash for cleaning yourself up after a big meal.

Here's what barbecue sauce can do for you:
- Make good barbecue look better
- Make good barbecue taste better
- Enhance the flavor of non barbecue foods or combinations of barbecue and non barbecue foods

Here's what barbecue sauce cannot do for you:
- Convert bad barbecue into good barbecue; if the barbecue is bad, throw it out!
- Erase wrinkles. It can please your palate, but it is not a wonder drug.
- Substitute fake barbecue for real barbecue. The secret to some barbecue may be in the sauce, but if the meat hasn't been cooked with the direct action of fire and smoke, it isn't barbecue.

Now that you know what you need and what sauce can and can't do for you, the following tips will help you maximize your pleasures with the nectar of the pit gods:

1. Pay attention to ingredients. If you are allergic to monosodium glutamate (MSG), for example, you should know that it isn't always listed as MSG (see the glossary). If you are allergic to fish, you should know that most true Worcestershire sauces contains anchovies. Many barbecue sauces contain Worcestershire sauce. If you are limiting your sodium intake, check the nutrition information on the sauce label. There is an extreme variance in different barbecue sauce brands' sodium content.

2. Don't burn your sauce. A common misuse of barbecue sauce is to put it on meat too early in the cooking process. You can use a vinegar-based sauce throughout the cooking process, but if the base or additional ingredients include tomato, corn syrup, or other sweeteners, the sauce can caramelize and burn on the meat. As a rule of thumb, brush sauce on the meat during the last fifteen to twenty minutes of cooking.

3. A little bit of sauce goes a long way. Moderation, as Pythagoras taught us, is good. When cooks serve me barbecue that is drowned in sauce, I wonder what they are trying to cover up. Too much sauce will overpower the flavor of the meat. The sauce should complement the meat's flavor. Put

a container of sauce on the table, for your guests to add more if they wish.

4. Serve sauce warm or at room temperature. Plan ahead if you're going to serve a sauce that you have stored in the refrigerator. Gently warm it before serving, or at least let it sit out long enough to reach room temperature.

5. Be creative. Put sauce in a plastic squeeze bottle and "paint" it on the serving plate and on the meat with squiggles or lines or other patterns. You'll get the best results with smooth sauces; chunky sauces may clog the nipple of the squeeze bottle. Besides creative presentations, try new and unusual uses for barbecue sauces in recipes. See the recipe for barbecue spaghetti, pig cigars, or Carolina paella in this book, for example.

Now you're ready to begin the adventure. Sit up straight, fasten your sauce belt, and prepare to have fun.

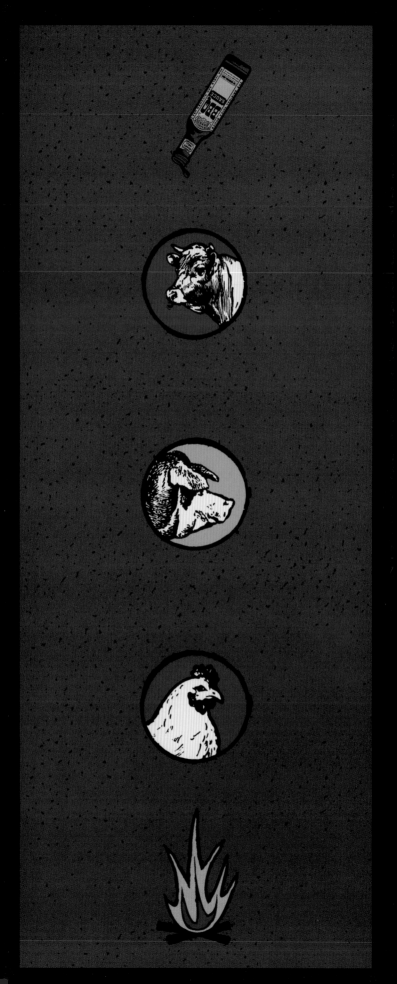

PART ONE

SAUCES

SWEET SAUCES

AMERICAN SPOON MANGO BBQ GRILLING SAUCE

PETOSKEY, MICHIGAN

Made for brushing on grilled foods before and/or during grilling, I recommend American Spoon Mango BBQ Grilling Sauce as a superb dipping sauce with chicken and pork. The blend of mango, brown sugar, pineapple juice, curry spices, and chile peppers is perfectly balanced to deliver tropical sweetness tempered with a tangy, spicy touch of fire.

ANDERSON'S BAR-B-Q SAUCE

MANHATTAN, KANSAS

Mitch Anderson's grandmother, Bessie Holland, taught Mitch a lot about cooking while he was growing up in North Carolina. Bessie was known throughout Bertie County for her culinary expertise. Now Mitch lives in Manhattan, Kansas, where he is an animal science technician at Kansas State University. He is also a barbecue sauce entrepreneur with ambitions to sell his sauces in the international marketplace. Mitch developed the sauce when he and his wife, Annette, ran out of sauce for a meat loaf one night and decided to make their own. After a lot of experimentation, the result was Anderson's Bar-B-Q Sauce. Anderson's Mild is a sweet, peppery, tomato-based sauce with a kiss of garlic and hickory smoke. The Cajun carries the flavors of the mild with a bite from red pepper. He also makes a Mesquite and a Jalapeño barbecue sauce. Anderson's Bar-B-Q Sauces are excellent as finishing sauces or dipping sauces on ribs, beef, chicken, and nonbarbecue foods such as meat loaf.

ANNIE'S BBQ SAUCE
NORTH CALAIS, VERMONT

Annie's will give a pleasant surprise to people who don't think of Vermont as a place to find good barbecue sauce. Built on a traditional foundation of tomato, vinegar, Worcestershire, and spices, and blended in its own way with some unique ingredients, Annie's delivers a sweet and tangy flavor with a hint of vegetarian Worcestershire and a pleasant peppery finish. My favorite is the Smokey Maple barbecue sauce, which enhances the great original recipe with the addition of maple syrup and maple smoke flavor.

ARBOR HILL SHERRIED WINE BARBEQUE SAUCE
NAPLES, NEW YORK

Arbor Hill delivers gourmet flavor with class. Sweet golden cream sherry, cane sugar, and honey are perfectly balanced with spicy mustard, soy sauce, and garlic. Arbor Hill is fabulous as a finishing and dipping sauce with pork, chicken, turkey, duck, and fish.

BABY JOE'S BBQ SAUCE
CARY, ILLINOIS

There really is a Baby Joe. He is a chef named Joe Kocher. Joe is head cook of the award-winning Baby Joe's Barbecue Cooking Team from suburban Chicago. Joe and his three associates—Joe Patricoski, Andy Rick, and Rick Dipper—have been so successful with their cooking and sauce at competitions around the country that they decided to put the sauce on the market. Your first taste will tell you why Baby Joe's BBQ Sauce is a winner. The slightly thin texture is just right for use as a finishing sauce or a dipping sauce. Baby Joe's sweetness is balanced perfectly with the tanginess of a spicy tomato base accented with hickory smoke.

BILARDO BROTHERS OF KANSAS CITY BARBECUE SAUCE

KANSAS CITY, MISSOURI

Thank goodness the Bilardo family decided to apply their artistic talents to the art of barbecue. This is a family gifted with illustrators, musicians, and cooks. Guided by Grandma Bilardo's admonition—"If you love to eat, you learn to cook"—they learned to cook. Their award-winning sauces are proof that they learned well. The original flavor is a thick, savory tomato-based sauce with a little bit of tanginess, a dash of sweetness, and a balanced blend of secret spices. The hot version will bite you, but it won't hurt. The sweetest sauce in the Bilardo line is Honey & Spice. It carries the signature flavors of the original, with extra measures of mustard and the addition of honey.

BLACKBURN'S PREMIUM MAPLE BARBECUE SAUCE

BRAMEN, MAINE

Stewart Blackburn has been to Memphis and other barbecue capitals, but that didn't deter him from developing a barbecue sauce with a Maine accent. Blackburn's Premium, developed when today's major barbecue cooking competitions were in the single digits, stands proudly among the best barbecue sauces. A tomato-based, thick, smooth sauce, textured with spices, Blackburn's has a rich, maple sweet, up-front introduction that is followed by a hit of garlic and a chile pepper finish. This sauce is a masterful combination for finishing or dipping with barbecued meats, and it's also great in barbecue beans.

BOARDROOM BAR-B-Q
ORIGINAL SAUCE
OVERLAND PARK, KANSAS

Scott O'Meara's barbecue hobby led him to the more serious business of making a living selling barbecue sauce and seasonings. Since Scott and his wife, Mary, opened Boardroom Bar-B-Q in 1991, it has become a mecca in the highly competitive Kansas City area barbecue market. Boardroom's red pepper bite is married to traditional spices, nested in molasses, and accented with garlic. Boardroom complements all of the basic barbecue food groups, especially pork ribs, beef brisket, and chicken wings. Mixed with Boardroom's Nuclear Chicken Wing seasoning, the original sauce is blasted into the fiery zone.

BOB SYKES BARB-Q SAUCE
BESSEMER, ALABAMA

This is an Alabama red sauce you'd best not be without. A worldwide family of friends recognizes the Bob Sykes signature on barbecue. You'll understand and join the family after bathing a bite or two of ribs in Bob Sykes BarB-Q Sauce. It is made to complement pork, chicken, and beef. The ingredients give a tip of the gimme cap to three Southern barbecue base traditions—vinegar, mustard, and tomato. The touch of Worcestershire sauce echoes colonial influences. Bob Sykes BarB-Q Sauce is smooth, mild, and gently spiced.

BODACIOUS VIDALIA BARBECUE SAUCE

WILLIAMSBURG, VIRGINIA

One thing struck me as curious about the Bodacious Vidalia Barbecue Sauce was the label. The Vidalia onions and sweet, fresh peaches pictured on the label are definitely associated with Georgia, yet the sauce is from Virginia. The explanation is that the sauce originated in Georgia. The producer, Peachtree Specialties, formerly of Atlanta, is now based in Williamsburg.

Bodacious Vidalia Barbecue Sauce doesn't contain peaches, but it does contain the famous sweet Vidalia onions. This smooth, full-bodied tomato-based sauce is Texas tangy and Georgia sweet, with a pleasing pepper finish. Bodacious Vidalia Barbecue Sauce is especially delicious on pulled pork, pork ribs, and beef brisket. The bodacious flavor should appeal to Texans, Georgians, Virginians, and many others.

BONE SUCKIN' SAUCE

RALEIGH, NORTH CAROLINA

Bone Suckin' suggests images of carnivores sitting around a campfire, devouring flamed meat with bone-sucking intensity. The sweet, spicy, vinegary aroma of Bone Suckin' Sauce is gentle to your nose. The sauce is thick enough to dance with meat yet thin enough to showcase the flakes of pepper and spices in burnt-orange puddles on your plate, your meat, your hands, your face. The sweet, tangy flavor does, as the label asserts, go well with an abundant variety of foods from surf, turf, barnyard, field, and orchard. An excellent all-around sauce, Bone Suckin' Sauce is a fabulous complement to barbecued pork butt, pork ribs, chicken, beef brisket, grilled veggie burgers, turkey, duck, rabbit, goat, and lamb. It's great, with bones or without!

BOOMER'S HEROES
ORIGINAL BBQ SAUCE
CINCINNATI, OHIO

Former Cincinnati Bengals quarterback "Boomer" Esiason didn't get his nickname on the football field. He earned it prenatally from his mother, due to his frequent kicking. The sauce that bears Norman Esiason Jr.'s nickname won't kick your palate, but the slight afterburn will please it. Tangy, slightly sweet, with a smoky, vinegar accent, this smooth, dark orange, tomato-based sauce is one of the best all-purpose mainstream barbecue finishing or dipping sauces on the market. It holds well to meat and complements all of the basic poultry, pork, and beef favorites of backyard pitmasters. Boomer's Heroes Original BBQ Sauce has also fared well in barbecue cooking competitions, where it was developed by the Texas Outlaws BBQ grilling team. Sawyer Industries produces it. Company president John Sawyer is co-founder and vice president of the Cincinnati Bengals. Part of the proceeds benefit the Heroes Foundation, for education and research about cystic fibrosis and an improved quality of life for people with cystic fibrosis. Boomer and Cheryl Esiason agreed to help market the sauce as a fundraiser after tasting it and market testing it themselves. The Gunnar H. Esiason Cystic Fibrosis and Lung Center is named after their son.

BROOK'S HOUSE
OF BAR-B-Q BEEF
AND PORK SAUCE
ONEONTA, NEW YORK

Residents of metropolitan Oneonta, New York, owe a heavy debt to chickens and eggs. The complete story of how Brook's House of Bar-B-Q started with chickens and eggs is too long to tell here. Briefly, however, it began in the 1950s, when Griffin Brooks and Frances McClelland fell in love, married, and bought her dad's chicken farm. More farms, chickens, eggs, children, and a barbecue catering business followed. When Griffin and Francis's son, John, and his wife, Joan, bought Brook's House of Bar-B-Q in 1975, it had grown to a 300-seat restaurant. Brook's continues to be a family-owned and operated business. I owe a heavy debt of gratitude to John and Joan's son, Ryan, for introducing me to Brook's House of Bar-B-Q Beef and Pork Sauce. He sent me a bottle, I tried it and loved it. Although this smooth, rich, lightly spiced sauce is sweet enough to eat with ice cream, it is an excellent complement to barbecued beef and pork. A barbecue cooking team from Massachusetts introduced me to Brook's House of Bar-B-Q Chicken Sauce. The tangy vinegar base with an herbal finish puts Brook's chicken sauce on the opposite end of the spectrum from sweet. It is fantastic as a marinade and mopping sauce with chicken and pork.

THE BROWN ADOBE
BARBECUE SAUCE
WILMINGTON, NORTH CAROLINA

As the name implies, this barbecue sauce with a "New Mexican connection" will complement your barbecue ribs, chicken, and grilled meats with the fresh salsa flavor of tomato, green and red chiles, vinegar, and spices. The Brown Adobe Barbecue Sauce was developed in New Mexico by Julienne Brown. Now owned by Wagner Gourmet Foods, Wilmington, North Carolina, this refreshingly different barbecue sauce is one of their top sellers. The Extra Spicy Brown Adobe adds a gentle fiery finish to the original flavor. Both are fabulous and versatile.

BUBBA BRAND WHITE
BARBEQUE SAUCE
CHARLESTON, SOUTH CAROLINA

Bubba Brand Bubba Q Sauce is a tangy vinegar and tomato-based sauce that excels at bringing out the flavor of barbecued pig meat. Bubba's pig pickin' parties wouldn't be complete without it.

Sometimes, however, Bubba departs from his pig pickin' ways and grills seafood. On those occasions he needs a more delicate sauce, which won't overpower the flavor of fish. That's what Bubba Brand White Barbeque Sauce does best. This thin orangish-white sauce with speckles of spices has a mellow, sweet mayonnaise flavor with a slight tang. Great as a basting and dipping sauce on seafood and chicken, this sauce also works well in potato salad, coleslaw, or green salad. It makes a great gift combo with tangy Bubba Brand Bubba Q Sauce.

BULL'S-EYE BARBECUE SAUCE
GARLAND, TEXAS

A few years ago, Bull's-Eye was the official barbecue sauce sponsor of Memphis in the May World Championship Barbecue Cooking Contest. I accepted a free sample from a young lady with a Memphis accent. I asked her, "What will I like about this sauce?" She didn't miss a beat in replying, "Big bold taste!" Yes, that's what she had been coached to say, but her reply was on target. I can still hear her say "Big bold taste!" each time I put Bull's-Eye on my barbecue. Now Bull's-Eye is a major player in the competitive barbecue sauce market. The thick, smooth, tomato-based sauce with a flawless balance of sweetness and spiciness puts a final touch on your palate with a kiss of hickory smoke. Bull's-Eye is remarkably good. It has earned its niche as one of America's favorite barbecue sauces. Variations from Bull's-Eye Original include Smokehouse Hickory, with more smoke flavor than the original flavor, and Raging Bull Spicy Hot, which is hot enough to burn but not hurt.

BUTCH'S BAR-B-Q SAUCE
ELLSWORTH, KANSAS

Each September at the Kansas State Fair in Hutchinson, Sidney W. "Butch" Lloyd and his family and helpers stay busier than a leisure suit at an Elvis convention. Sometimes the line is a block long at Butch's Bar-B-Q. Nevertheless, customers wait patiently in hot sun, driving rain, or balmy breezes. They know it's worth the wait. Kansans still take time to visit with one another, and visiting goes especially well when you're smelling sweet hickory smoke from Butch's pit. Butch's customers buy pit-smoked barbecued pork ribs, beef sandwiches, pork sandwiches, sausage sandwiches, and beefalo burgers, with sides of coleslaw, beans, or potato salad. Butch has catered since 1981. Butch knows his way around the pit and the sauce pot. Butch's Bar-B-Q Sauce evolved from experimenting and getting customer opinions of each batch. His customers demand a dark, tomato-based sauce, gently spiced, sweet and smoky, with a touch of tanginess. A little bit on your barbecue will make it rock 'n' roll.

CHARLIE BEIGG'S MAINE APPLE BBQ SAUCE
WINDHAM, MAINE

Although Charlie Beigg's Maine Apple BBQ Sauce is made in Maine, it has roots in a Kansas hog farm. Brian and Laura Stevens, husband-wife co-owners and operators of the Charlie Beigg's Restaurant in Windham, Maine, can trace some influence on their sauces to Brian's grandmother and grandfather, who operated a hog farm in Hoyt, Kansas. Brian says his grandmother was an excellent cook and a culinary inspiration to him. When Brian put his imagination to work with local Maine products, he came up with this excellent sauce. It clings well to the meat and delivers a pleasant, distinctive apple flavor nestled in a tomato base, sweetened with molasses, and touched with a complementary blend of secret spices. Other Charlie Beigg's sauces include a savory Hot Pepper Grilling & BBQ Sauce—spicy, slightly tangy, with a gentle kick from hot pepper—and a Bourbon BBQ & Grilling Sauce, sweeter and less tangy than the hot pepper flavor, with a subtle touch of bourbon. Some proceeds from the sale of these sauces benefit a local nonprofit organization that provides supportive housing and employment for persons with disabilities.

CHARLOTTE'S RIB
SPICY SOUTHERN

BALLWIN, MISSOURI

Herb "Dr. Rollin Rivers" Schwarz cooks barbecued ribs so well that you'll want more even when you're full. I know this because several years ago Dr. Rivers and I hit almost every rib joint in St. Louis in one afternoon and evening. We didn't just look and smell. We ate. When we ended our adventure at Charlotte's Rib for a ribcap (recap discussion of ribs eaten), I was so full I thought I couldn't look at another rib for at least a month. Herb brought me one anyway. I ate it. It was the best rib I'd had all day, so I ate another one. Part of Herb's award-winning secret is in his sauces. He makes four varieties of smooth, flavorful tomato-based sauces. My favorite is Spicy Southern, a tangy/sweet spicy tomato sauce with a pepper finish and a gentle bite. Western Blend is sweeter, less tangy, with a touch of maple flavor and a spicy finish, including a tinge of hot pepper. Mild Hickory is the original house sauce, with mellow Missouri sweetness and hickory smoke. Herb's new Lo-Cal is just in time for baby boomers who want full flavor with no guilt. Although low in sugar, sodium, and fat, Lo-Cal puts a full measure of sweet tomato spicy goodness on your ribs.

CHEF ALLEN'S PAPAYA
GRILLING SAUCE

NORTH MIAMI BEACH, FLORIDA

Chef Allen Susser has been long recognized as one of the leading chefs of the red hot South Florida culinary scene--along with the likes of Norman Van Aken and Mark Millitello. Chef Allen is a master of citrus and exotic fruit sauces, and this is only one of his many excellent and highly original blends. I would almost call this sauce "bright." The use of papaya blended with other exotic fruits makes for a vivid flavor that could work on a variety of foods, grilled, barbecued, or otherwise. Seafood absolutely glows when Chef Allen's is basted on as a finishing sauce. If you are looking for a truly different sauce, try his Mango Ketchup on a batch of french fries.

CHRISTOPHER RANCH
GARLIC B-B-Q SAUCE
GILROY, CALIFORNIA

If you can't go to the annual garlic festival in Gilroy, California, "The Garlic Capital of the World," console yourself with Christopher Ranch Garlic B-B-Q Sauce on a slab of barbecued pork ribs. Be advised: If you don't like garlic, please save this precious condiment for those who do. Christopher Ranch laces powerful hits of chopped, crunchy garlic throughout this robust nectar. The sweet, seasoned, tomato base lends a complementary balance. Try it with grilled chicken breast or as sauce on a grilled gourmet pizza. Other imaginative uses abound.

COACH SPOSATO'S
BAR-B-Q SAUCE
TULSA, OKLAHOMA

Sports took Coach Jim Sposato from his home state of New York to Oklahoma and Arkansas. Barbecue kept him there. He competes in at least fifteen barbecue cooking contests each year and frequently goes home with ribbons and trophies. Coach has developed a great all-purpose, all-American sweet, tomato-based barbecue sauce with a rich, smoky flavor that will help you score compliments in your neighborhood or points in a competition. Coach makes a gently All-American hot version of the milder Varsity sauce. Each bottle comes with practical "Que Tips" on the label.

COOKIES WESTERN STYLE
BAR "B" "Q" SAUCE
WALL LAKE, IOWA

The name provokes cognitive dissonance. We usually associate milk, not barbecue sauce, with cookies. They name it after its inventor, L. D. Cook, nicknamed "Cookie." Since its commercial debut in 1975, from a corner of the Wall Lake Fire Department garage, Cookies now occupies its own 65,000 square-foot production facility, complete with test kitchen. A giant among sauces in Iowa, Cookies captured Best Sauce on the Planet honors in Kansas City in 1996. I like the Western Style best. Its dark, thick tomato base delivers a tangy sweet complement to pork and chicken, with a spicy, but not fiery, cayenne pepper finish. Cookies Country Blend is tangier than the Western Style and doesn't bite.

CORKY'S
MEMPHIS, TENNESSEE

Corky's Bar-B-Q is to Memphis as Gates Bar-B-Q is to Kansas City. It is one of the most popular barbecue restaurants in town. Corky's differs from Gates in flavor, decor, service, and number of restaurants. There's only one Corky's and several Gates. Corky's sauce is the next best thing to a visit to the restaurant on Poplar Avenue in Memphis. The aroma shouts "barbecue!" the instant you open the bottle. This dark red, smooth tomato-based sauce is sweet, but still has the mid-South touch of vinegar blended with smoke, pepper, and a hint of hot pepper.

THE COUNTY LINE
BARBEQUE BAR-B-Q SAUCE
AUSTIN, TEXAS

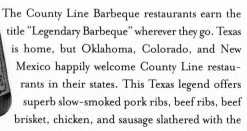

The County Line Barbeque restaurants earn the title "Legendary Barbeque" wherever they go. Texas is home, but Oklahoma, Colorado, and New Mexico happily welcome County Line restaurants in their states. This Texas legend offers superb slow-smoked pork ribs, beef ribs, beef brisket, chicken, and sausage slathered with the signature County Line sauce. County Line's Original sauce is thin, smooth, slightly sweet, with a spicy, smoky, full-bodied

flavor and a touch of vinegar. They make the sauce to complement the full repertoire of barbecue meats served at the restaurants, and it does so with excellence. The Wild Pork Sauce is
spicier and sweeter than the original. Hot and Spicy is a full-
flavored variation of the original with a tolerable level of fire.

COWBOY MARINADE
BARBECUE SAUCE
HIGHLAND PARK, ILLINOIS

When you're almost finished grilling a burger or barbecuing a beef brisket, grab a bottle of Cowboy Marinade
Barbecue Sauce. This thick, spicy sauce with a tangy,
sweet tomato flavor should be applied to barbecued
or grilled meats the last ten or fifteen minutes of
cooking. Try it on your barbecued ribs and chicken
or use it as a table sauce. Market Square Food Company sells the sauce separately, or in attractive "saddle bags" with a bag of Cowboy Snack Mix.

COWGIRL BRAND BELLE'S
BAR-B-QUE SAUCE
BARTLESVILLE, OKLAHOMA

Presented as a sauce worthy of cowgirls, Belle's Bar-B-
Que Sauce works well as a finishing or dipping sauce
with beef, pork, and chicken. Thick enough to stick
to meat, Belle's tomato ketchup-based sweetness is
tempered with Worcestershire sauce, lemon juice,
black pepper, and hickory smoke. The black pepper hits first, followed by sweetness, and finished
with a gentle cayenne fire.

CRAZY CHARLEY CAJUN SAUCE

COBB, CALIFORNIA

Brewed coffee is a major ingredient in the Crazy Charley rendition of Cajun All-Purpose & BBQ Sauce. Coffee does not, however, dominate the flavor. Tomato ketchup and brown sugar add sweetness. Worcestershire sauce, vinegar, mustard, onion, garlic, and some secret spices add flavor, and Tabasco brand hot pepper sauce imparts a Cajun accent. Gumbo filé is one of the thickeners. Charley's recipe is adapted from one his sister gave him. She got it as a thank-you gift from a Cajun grandmother, who in turn had gotten it from her grandmother. "The Sauce" is a sweet, spicy complement to barbecued pork, beef, chicken, and alligator. It clings well to meat, and is useful in a variety of nonbarbecue foods, such as meat loaf and beans. Crazy Charley also makes an excellent hot version of the original.

CRAZY JIM'S BARBEQUE SAUCE

WHITE HORSE BEACH, MASSACHUSETTS

We can thank Jim Igo, a mail carrier and accomplished pit-master, for inventing Crazy Jim's Barbeque Sauce. Crazy Jim's is chunky, slightly thick, molasses dark with sweet, almost fruity, overtones. The combination of wine vinegar tanginess is balanced just right with sweetness. Cayenne and chile peppers give this sauce a gently fiery accent that will warm your tongue, but won't hurt you. Crazy Jim's Hot & Spicy won Best Sauce on the Planet, 1997, at the American Royal in Kansas City.

CURLEY'S FAMOUS HICKORY BARBECUE SAUCE

HUTCHINSON, KANSAS

Curley's has been an award-winning favorite in Kansas for many years. Curley's Hickory is a sweet and tangy, smooth, tomato-based sauce with a smoky, spicy finish and a hint of garlic and onion. Curley's Smoky is similar to Hickory, with more smoke flavor. Curley's Mesquite substitutes mesquite smoke flavor for the original hickory. Curley's Hot & Spicy is spicier and adds a medium hit of red pepper fire. Curley's Honey Dijon is the most pronounced departure from the original Hickory. Sweetened Dijon mustard is the signature flavor in this wonderful, thick barbecue sauce. Curley's excels on beef brisket, hamburgers, pork burgers, and in baked beans. Try Honey Dijon in pork sandwiches and chicken.

DADDY JACK'S BBQ SAUCE

WICHITA, KANSAS

The rib-bearing jalapeño pepper on Daddy Jack's label wears a lip-smacking friendly smile. A bit of Daddy Jack's BBQ Sauce on *your* ribs can give you a lip-smacking smile too. Jalapeño peppers are part of the secret. There's just enough jalapeño to tingle on your lips, not burn you. The flavor of Daddy Jack's benefits from a balanced mix of tomato, peppers, spices, sweetness, and tanginess. A popular sauce in its birthplace, Wichita, Kansas, Daddy Jack's BBQ Sauce is attracting a widening circle of friends and customers in the Midwest and beyond.

DAVID'S REAL PIT BBQ SAUCE

GAINESVILLE, FLORIDA

David's Gainsesville, Florida, restaurant is billed as "The Best BBQ South of the Mason-Dixon Line." The sauce—sold from the restaurant and by way of the Internet—will give you an inkling of how good David's barbecue must be. David's Original is a dark, smooth, tomato-based balance of sweet, tart, and spicy, accented with smoke flavor. For a kick in the taste buds, try David's Original Hot. David's Hickory Sweet recipe is a sweeter, thicker version of the original flavor. All three sauces are excellent complements to ribs, beef, chicken, and more.

DEAN & DANNY'S RAMBLIN ROADHOUSE BBQ SAUCE

THOUSAND OAKS, CALIFORNIA

The legend about the creation of Dean & Danny's Ramblin Roadhouse BBQ Sauce involves a truck full of livestock colliding with a truck full of firewood and a truck full of produce. Fire from mesquite made barbecue of the livestock and a gourmet sauce out of the produce. The legend is a stretch of the imagination, but the sauce is real and powerful. Dean & Danny's thick, rich, peppery, sweet tomato-based flavor, with a little bit of vinegar and lemon juice tanginess, is made to complement beef, pork, chicken, and other meats.

DINOSAUR BAR-B-QUE SENSUOUS SLATHERING SAUCE

SYRACUSE, NEW YORK

For years I've contended that barbecuers were the original philosophers. Prehistoric pitmasters sat around the campfire, eating the flame-cooked kill of the day, while discussing the meaning of life. That, I've speculated, is where we got the expression, "I have a bone to pick with you." When Wild Oats Community Market opened a store in my neighborhood, I found the perfect sauce to go with the story. I met Dinosaur Bar-B-Que Sensuous Slathering Sauce and have kept it stocked in my cupboard and refrigerator ever since. I keep it because it's a darned good sauce; however, that it fits my story is a happy coincidence. John Stage, principal owner of Dinosaur Bar-B-Que, in Syracuse, New York, may offer other reasons for the name, but I'm sticking to my story. In the crowded field of tomato-based barbecue sauces, Dinosaur makes an aggressive statement of Jurassic proportions. Spicy, tangy, sweet, and complex—the flavor of Dinosaur can't be found in any other bottle. Go to the "Fiery" section of this book for a review of Dinosaur Wango Tango Bar-B-Que Sauce.

DREAMCATCHER BLACK CHERRY BAR-B-QUE SAUCE

ONEKAMA, MICHIGAN

Master Chef Raymond Shonk adds a generous serving of black cherries to a tomato base and some other familiar barbecue sauce ingredients in his imaginative Dreamcatcher Black Cherry Bar-B-Que Sauce. The result is a fresh, sweet, fabulous flavor that complements fish, chicken, turkey, beef, pork, and wild game. With its smooth texture, this sauce works well as a finishing sauce and dipping sauce.

EL PASO CHILE COMPANY DARK SECRET MOLE

EL PASO, TEXAS

Thick, rich, and complex, with a refreshing balance of tomato ketchup, roasted chile peppers, cocoa, molasses, and spices, El Paso Chile Company's Dark Secret Mole is outstanding with grilled or barbecued chicken.

FAT DADDY & OLD WOMAN BAR-B-Q SAUCE

ARKANSAS CITY, KANSAS

Although people say that Chester Barton looks like Santa Claus, he's more comfortable with the name "Fat Daddy." When he was competing in a barbecue cooking contest years ago in Perry, Oklahoma, he found out that he couldn't call his team "Fat Daddy" because another team was registered as "Fat Daddy." He decided to figure out a new name while sipping a cool beverage. When he said to his wife, "Old woman, bring me something to drink," the name for a team, restaurant, and barbecue sauce was born. The name has served Chester and Francis Barton well. They have a loyal base of customers in southern Kansas and northern Oklahoma, and they often attract travelers on the name alone.

What Fat Daddy & Old Woman Bar-B-Q Sauce lacks in political correctness, it compensates for in flavor. The original old family recipe from which it was derived was too sweet for the local palate, so Chester experimented until he got it right. Some of the experiments were so bad that even the dog wouldn't eat them. In the end, Fat Daddy perfected a smooth, tomato-based sauce, sprinkled with tiny pieces of onion, flecks of black pepper, and hot pepper seeds. It is slightly sweet and spicy, with a gentle bite at the finish. Fiery eaters will love the Hot and Extra Hot. Fat Daddy may not be Santa Claus, but his sauce is gifted enough to make him the Saint Nicholas of the Barbecue Pits.

FLOWER OF THE FLAMES ORIGINAL BAR-B-Q SAUCE

LENEXA, KANSAS

Karen Putnam's red hair, culinary magic with fire, and queenly style earned her the title "Flower of the Flames" in 1985. Cooking with her husband, Jim "Putter," and other relatives and friends, her teams have won hundreds of barbecue cooking contest awards, including world championships. It is no surprise, therefore, that she makes world-class barbecue sauces.

Karen's original sauce is a sweet, flavorful balance of complementary spices, with a hint of celery and a peppery afterglow, in a tomato base. Raspberry combines the classic flavors of the original in a sweet tomato and raspberry base. Fire eaters will want Hot & Sassy Raspberry. The Flower of the Flames repertoire also includes a fantastic sweet and spicy Gourmet Honey & Spice, a Honey Mustard with a tangy, sweet, spicy balance that will do a Georgia hog proud, and a better-than-ketchup delicious Candice's Kid's Que for kids of any age.

GENO'S PREMIUM BARBECUE SAUCE

EL CAJON, CALIFORNIA

Gene "Geno" Jenkins likes to emphasize that Geno's Premium Barbecue Sauce doesn't "overpower the flavor of the meat!" Another difference Geno emphasizes is the absence of hickory smoke, garlic, vinegar, or ketchup flavors in his barbecue sauces. For best results, Geno recommends dipping barbecue meats in a bowl of Geno's Premium Barbecue Sauce after you have cooked the meat. This will bring out the full flavor of the meat—be it pork, chicken, beef, or another meat. I like to pour a puddle of Geno's on my plate and dip each bite in it as I eat. Geno makes a mild sauce, a spicy sauce, and a hot sauce. Geno's spicy sauce delivers a spicy finish to the mellow flavor of the original mild. The hot version of the same basic recipe will bite you, especially if you cook with it.

GOODE COMPANY BBQ HALL OF FLAME BBQ SAUCE

HOUSTON, TEXAS

Longnecks are at home at a rodeo, a cowboy's campfire, and a Texas-style bodaciously big barbecue. It's a stroke of genius, therefore, that Jim Goode bottles his Goode Company BBQ Hall of Flame BBQ Sauce in a longneck. Unlike beer, however, you don't want to serve this sauce chilled. It's good enough to drink from the longneck, but it really belongs on your meat. It's best when heated then dripped over mesquite-smoked beef brisket, pork spare ribs, or hot links. The thin, orange-colored liquid, flecked with onion, pepper, and herbs, lends a gentle, slightly sweet, savory complement to meat that has been cooked to perfection and doesn't need a zesty kick. Goode Company sauce gives a pleasant peppery aftertaste that stokes your hunger for more. Two variations, Jalapeño and Honey Garlic, take the original flavor on a wild ride to cowboy heaven.

HAPPY "HOLLA" BAR-B-Q SAUCE
SHAWNEE MISSION, KANSAS

Ed Roith is known from Maynard, Massachusetts, to Terlingua, Texas, for his winning ways with barbecue. Ed cooks barbecue, eats barbecue, and teaches barbecue in person and on video all over the country. He also makes sauce and rubs that will serve you well in barbecue competition and for home entertainment. Happy "Holla" is a mythical place where cheerful pigs dressed in overalls and cowboy hats play fiddles and dance a pig jig. It is a fitting name for the sauce because Happy "Holla" dances well with pigs. Happy "Holla" is smooth, sweet and spicy, in a tomato base with a subtle garlic finish. The hot version bites you gently. Excellent for finishing or dipping on pig and all other varieties of barbecued meat, and as a flavor enhancer in beans and meat loaf.

HAWAIIAN PLANTATIONS MAUI ONION
HONOLULU, HAWAII

Hawaiian Plantations Maui Onion uses fresh Hawaiian produce to a "que"linary advantage. Crushed pineapple, sweet Maui onions, orange peel, and honey are blended with tomato, spices, and kiawe smoke flavor to create an exceptional barbecue sauce. Kiawe's nickname is "Hawaiian Mesquite." Textured with minced Maui onions, the sweet, tangy flavor of Hawaiian Plantations Maui Onion is spicy up front, with a touch of smoke at the finish. Hawaiian Plantations puts an extra measure of kiawe (pronounced "key-ah-vey") smoke in their Kiawe Smoke BBQ Sauce. This sauce also contains crushed pineapple. It is smooth, sweet, spicy, and smoky. Both are excellent sauces. My favorite is Maui Onion; it will earn a place on your table.

HEAD COUNTRY
BAR-B-Q SAUCE
PONCA CITY, OKLAHOMA

Born in a land where the clay earth is Tuscany red, where oil wells are as common as cowboy boots, and where the Hereford is king, Head Country Bar-B-Q Sauce could be called "essence of Oklahoma." True to Southwestern cattle ranch tradition, it is tomato-based and accented with vinegar, sugar, and secret spices. Starting with his Uncle Bud and Aunt Frieda's original recipe, Danny Head, his wife Carey, and a loyal team of pitmasters have brought Head Country from local popularity to international fame. Head Country is a winner at sauce contests and cooking contests around the world. Head Country Original is a perfect blend of spicy sweetness. As the Head family says, "One taste will hook you!" Two variations of the original— Hickory Smoke and Hot—round out the Head Country medley. Use Head Country on barbecued beef, pork, chicken, and barbecued baloney—an Oklahoma favorite.

HILLSDALE BANK
BAR-B-Q SAUCE
HILLSDALE, KANSAS

The original Hillsdale Bank in Hillsdale, Kansas, opened in 1906 and closed in 1930. Greg and Donna Beverlin converted it into a barbecue restaurant in 1989. It's a comfortable, nostalgic setting for swine dining. Rural and metro Kansas City-area residents break ribs together at Hillsdale Bank Bar-B-Q. The hickory-smoked meats are excellent and so is The Sauce. Smooth, full-bodied, and tomato-based, The Sauce complements your barbecue with Kansas City sweetness, Tennessee tanginess, and Texas smoke and pepper. And it's reasonably priced, worth your investment. A phone call to Greg or Donna will get you direct access to "The Sauce."

HOG HEAVEN SOOEE SAUCE
VIRGINIA BEACH, VIRGINIA

Hog Heaven Sooee Sauce is a delicious tomato-based sweet and tangy sauce with a spicy finish, excellent on all parts of barbecued hog as a finishing or dipping sauce. It's also great with chicken as well as grilled beef steaks, pork chops, fish, and shrimp. Hog Heaven Habañero Hot is the Sooee Sauce of choice for fiery eaters.

HOGWASH
RICHARDSON, TEXAS

"Hogwash!" you may say when told that a unique mixture of brown sugar, lemon juice, horseradish, and secret spices can enhance the flavor of your barbecue. Although its creators at Ham I Am!, in Richardson, Texas, say Hogwash is "good on practically everything," it usually shares retail shelf space with barbecue sauces. Stretch yourself and try this extraordinary marriage of sweet, savory, and tangy flavors on your ribs and shoulders.

HOLLYWOOD CHICKEN
HOMESTYLE BBQ SAUCE
OAKLAND, CALIFORNIA

This sauce comes in three varieties—Mild, Hot, and Honey Mustard. The mild and hot are tomato-based, smooth textured, and laced with Worcestershire sauce, cayenne pepper sauce, chile powder, herbs, and spices to gently complement your backyard barbecued meats. Both sauces are good as finishing sauces applied during the last fifteen to thirty minutes of cooking, and as dipping sauces. Hollywood Chicken Hot delivers a medium swift kick of hot pepper. My favorite is the Hollywood Chicken Honey Mustard. The sweet, smooth, orangish-yellow combination of ballpark mustard with tomato purée and chile powder spiciness gives the right touch to ribs, pork, chicken, grilled burgers, brats, hot dogs, and more.

HONEYCUP BBQ SAUCE
SADDLE BROOK, NEW JERSEY

The attractive faceted glass bottle, labeled with gold, is too fancy for an ordinary sauce. Honeycup BBQ Sauce is not an ordinary sauce. Although it is sweet enough to live up to its name, its sweetness is contrasted with tanginess, spices, and a kiss of hickory smoke. Ribs, chicken, pork, and veal respond well to Honeycup BBQ Sauce at the finish or for dipping.

IRON HORSE FARM BAR-B-QUE SAUCE
GALVA, KANSAS

The label will pique your curiosity. Why is an old green and yellow tractor—originally nicknamed, "iron horse"—on a barbecue sauce label? The intended connection is between a farmer's smile and the flavor of the sauce. The sound of an old "Johnnie Popper"—a tractor in vogue from 1929 to 1935, when commercially bottled barbecue sauce was in its infancy—brings a smile to the farmer's face: The "fine flavor" of the sauce brings a smile to your face.

Iron Horse Farm Bar-B-Que Sauce is produced by Darryl Unruh in the rural community of Galva, Kansas. Darryl's original recipe sauce is as sweet as a first kiss in the tunnel of love at the state fair. Trying the sauce on a variety of meats and other foods is as fun as a stroll down the midway. The first surge of sweetness is followed by a gentle, tangy bite of pepper and vinegar.

Iron Horse Farm is excellent on beef, chicken, and pork. A dash or two on a pork barbecue sandwich from Galva's local barbecue restaurant, and you'll want to move to Kansas—or return often enough to qualify for frequent farmer credits.

D.L. JARDINE'S CAMPFIRE HICKORY FLAVOR BAR-B-Q SAUCE

BUDA, TEXAS

D. L. Jardine's Campfire Hickory Flavor Bar-B-Q Sauce is an excellent example of the classic American tomato-based barbecue sauce. Jardine's enhances rich tomato flavor with pepper, smoke, and sweetness. This is a great all-around finishing and dipping sauce for any barbecued or grilled meats. For a similar flavor with a Texas mesquite accent, try Jardine's Mesquite Bar-B-Q Sauce.

JOHNNY D'S BARBEQUE COMPANY GIMME DAT BARBEQUE AND DIPPING SAUCE

LOS ALAMITOS, CALIFORNIA

Johnny D's commands your attention. It jumps out at you with a delightful burst of garlic, orange, pepper, and mysterious signature spices. The spicy version tickles your mouth with fire. True to the promise on the label, Johnny D's "grandad's special recipe" gives a special accent to chicken, beef, pork, or fish. It's also a great multipurpose condiment. Johnny D's turf or surf marinades and mopping sauces include a poultry Bird Bath, beef Angus Stock, pork Hawg Wash, and fish Shark Bait. Each is outstanding. I like them equally well as dipping sauces—on their designated meats and on other meats. Angus Stock will tame wild boar, pheasant, and venison.

JOHNNY'S BAR-B-Q

MISSION, KANSAS

When Johnny White converted a former Mission, Kansas, pizza shop into Johnny's Bar-B-Q in 1977, it didn't take long for the sweet smell of hickory smoke to lure thousands of customers. And they keep coming back. Although a bottle of Johnny's sauce won't give you the ambiance or hustle and bustle of his dining room, it will be friendly to your meat. Johnny's uncomplicated sweet and spicy blend of tomato, sugar, vinegar, salt, and signature spices that smack of cinnamon and allspice is great on ribs, pork, chicken, turkey, sausage, fries, omelettes, and more.

KC MASTERPIECE
OAKLAND, CALIFORNIA

This sauce has already won, hands down, the award for "BBQ Sauce Phenomenon of the Twentieth Century." In a century dominated by a few big brand names, a new tomato-based, molasses-sweetened flavor was developed in a suburban Midwestern kitchen by Dr. Rich Davis, a child psychiatrist and barbecue hobbyist. It emerged as a giant among sauces, a household name, and a better-than-ketchup all-purpose condiment. From the original molasses-sweet, tomato-based sauce, with a palate-pleasing, complex, full-bodied blend of secret spices, KC Masterpiece has spun off a variety of other flavors, including Honey Dijon. The latter is especially good with chicken and pork. The original is good with anything.

KHATSA TIBETAN BARBECUE MARINADE
BELLEVUE, WASHINGTON

Khatsa promises to "liberate your senses." Although Khatsa contains seven of the most popular barbecue sauce ingredients in America, it takes customary American barbecue flavor in an entirely new direction. Caraway seeds, ginger, chiles, and toasted soybeans help make the difference. The Kyaping family, creators of this nutty, grainy nectar laced with garlic, call their barbecue sauce a marinade. It does an admirable job as a chicken, pork, and seafood marinade and excels as a dipping sauce with barbecued pork and chicken.

Tsetan Kyaping developed the signature flavors of Khatsa sauces while he was a political prisoner in a Tibetan prison for two decades and worked as a cook. His daughter, Dachen, helped adapt Tsetan's Tibetan dry spice blends into a liquid that would appeal to American palates. Dachen, a commercial artist, also designed the imaginative Khatsa labels. Besides barbecue sauce, they make Khatsa Tibetan Hot Sauce and Khatsa Tibetan Salsa. The name *Khatsa* means "hot mouth." The barbecue sauce, however, is mild. It won't burn your mouth. Besides barbecue, Khatsa barbecue sauce is great in stir-fry with vegetables, tofu, pork, chicken, or beef. The Kyaping family donates some of the profits from this fantastic sauce to World Concern, a Seattle-based conservation and education organization that has projects in the Mt. Everest area and in Tibet.

LAST ROUNDUP
BARBEQUE SAUCE
SAN DIEGO, CALIFORNIA

When Eric Rein and his family moved from Kansas City to San Diego several years ago, they couldn't find a barbecue sauce that tasted like home. They decided to make their own. Last Roundup is the result, says Eric, of their "long, arduous journey of designing and fine-tuning, with endless sampling." The Rein family has done an excellent job of creating a traditional yet unique, sweet, tangy, smoky, spicy, tomato-based barbecue sauce. The uniqueness stems from their use of nontraditional Asian and Jamaican spices, which make the sauce more complex and full-bodied. Use it on chicken, turkey, pork, ribs, brisket, and burgers. Also good with fries or pan-fried potatoes. Eric says another use is for "the best Sloppy Joe you've ever tasted."

LEA & PERRINS
BARBECUE SAUCE

FAIR LAWN, NEW JERSEY

As a name for a barbecue sauce, Lea & Perrins is a rel-
ative newcomer. Lea & Perrins Worcestershire Sauce,
however, is a familiar, popular, widely used seasoning for steaks, meat loaf, soups, and many other
food dishes. It is a key ingredient in hundreds of
barbecue sauces. The smooth, rich, molasses-
darkened tomato base of Lea & Perrins Barbecue
Sauce, accented with Worcestershire sauce, hickory smoke, and secret spices, delivers a classic American barbecue sauce flavor to all barbecued meats. Lea & Perrins Barbecue Sauce, like their famous Worcestershire sauce, will serve
a multitude of future generations.

LEE KUM KEE CHINESE
CHAR SIU SAUCE

HONG KONG, CHINA/ALHAMBRA, CALIFORNIA

Lee Kum Kee's signature flavors of soy sauce,
ginger, garlic, honey, and secret spices come
through to perfection in their Chinese Char
Siu Sauce. Too thick and salty to use for dipping, it is still an excellent complement to
grilled chicken or barbecued pork ribs when
brushed on the last few minutes of cooking. It is also handy
for stir-fry, with vegetables, beef, chicken, pork, or shrimp.

LEGEND HEARTLAND
BARBECUE SAUCE

CHICAGO, ILLINOIS

Legend sauces are produced by Seasons Harvest,
Inc., Chicago. Company founder Charles Moore
has used recipes from his mother and grandmother as the basis for the Legend sauces. Photo por-
traits on the labels are Moore family relatives.

Heartland tastes as fresh as if it came directly
from grandma's kitchen. Thick, textured with

bits of onion, pineapple, and raisins in a tomato base, Heartland delivers a wholesome, slightly smoky barbecue complement, with a gentle bite at the finish. Heartland is excellent on
ribs, chicken, and beef.

Legend Southwest Barbecue Sauce is a smooth, thick,
smoky, tomato-based sauce with a touch of Southwestern
spices. Dip with ribs, chicken, and brisket.

LIL JAKE'S KANSAS CITY BARBECUE SAUCE

KANSAS CITY, MISSOURI

A taste of Kansas City barbecue history, this sauce has
been pit nectar to several generations. Simple and
direct, it is a smooth, flavorful blend of tomato
ketchup, water, sugar, and spices. Son of the late,
legendary Jake Edwards, Danny, "Lil Jake," still
makes it the way Dad did. You can get it down-
town at Danny's Lil Jake's Eat It and Beat It
barbecue establishment. Lil Jake's Barbecue
Sauce gives the sweet and spicy side of Kansas City's accent to
your beef, pork, and chicken. For fire, sprinkle meat with hot
pepper before adding the sauce. Danny offers African bird
pepper at the restaurant. A little bit will ignite your tongue.
More will beat it into orbit.

THE LOLLIPOP TREE TRIPLE PEPPER GRILLING & BASTING SAUCE

PORTSMOUTH, NEW HAMPSHIRE

Unless you've licked one of "Crazy Sam" Higgins's
Texas Jalapeño Lollipops, you expect pure sweetness from a sauce made by a company called "The
Lollipop Tree." Just like Sam's lollipop, however, your first bite of Triple Pepper Grilling &
Basting Sauce will soothe your palate with the
pleasure of fire and sweetness. Being from New
Hampshire, the Lollipop Tree combination of fire and sweet
is milder than Texas versions, but you won't argue with it. You

shouldn't peg Triple Pepper as "strictly Yankee" because of its origin. Its triple combination of sweet and hot peppers and spices could be comfortably at home in a Southern picnic or on a Midwestern farm table. Medium red, with a smooth glazed texture, speckled with peppers and pepper seeds, this sauce is as pleasing to look at as to taste. In a former life they labeled it "ketchup." It is versatile enough to work as ketchup, barbecue dipping sauce, grilling sauce, meat loaf enhancer, taco or fajita dressing, or with Chinese sweet-and-sour dishes.

LUM TAYLOR'S SECRET RECIPE RIVERBOAT STYLE BARBEQUE SAUCE

EVANSTON, ILLINOIS

Adrien "Lum" Taylor Sr. had two passions: paddle-wheel riverboats and cooking. He made a living as a boat and barge mechanic in the Madison, Indiana, area. More important to us, however, he developed a recipe for a barbecue baste. Lum Sr. passed his secret basting recipe along to his son, Adrien "Lum" Taylor Jr., who refined it into today's product. Ronald Taylor, son of Lum Taylor Jr., is now the keeper of the recipe. John T. Bianucci, president of World Wide Food Products, persuaded Ron Taylor to put the sauce on the market. Lum Taylor's Secret Recipe Riverboat Style Barbecue Sauce is a marriage of Northern sweetness and spicy Southern tanginess. Hot sauce, cayenne pepper, and red pepper flakes add a gentle fiery finish to this fabulous, versatile sauce. If you like sweet sauce, Lum Taylor's will float your boat.

HISTORIC LYNCHBURG, TENNESSEE WHISKEY BARBECUE SAUCE

LYNCHBURG, TENNESSEE

If there ever was a Norman Rockwell America, it is still happening in Lynchburg, Tennessee. Red brick buildings, brick paving, porched sidewalks, friendly people, and old-time products for sale give you the feel that you've stepped back in time. Various foods in Lynchburg contain a touch of "the local product," Jack Daniel's whiskey. Naturally, there's a barbecue sauce flavored with the local product. Mr. Daniel was known to like barbecue. The Lynchburg Merchandise Company, in cooperation with Ron Boyle, of Porky's Products, took an old family recipe dating five generations back, to the turn of the century, and perfected a sweet, tomato-based, whiskey-kissed sauce that Mr. Daniel would be proud to call his own. The sauce comes in "poofs" ranging from Sweet `N Mild (86 Poof) to Fiery Smokin' Hot (151 Poof!). The Jack Daniel's distillery is not associated with the manufacture of the sauce. Historic Lynchburg Tennessee Whiskey Barbecue Sauce, a sweet and spicy tomato-based finishing or dipping sauce, will complement all of your favorite barbecue foods. Find the poof that best suits you, and keep a supply on hand. You'll love it.

MAPLE GROVE FARMS OF VERMONT HONEY MUSTARD SAUCE
ST. JOHNSBURY, VERMONT

Maple Grove Farms of Vermont has established a conspicuous presence on supermarket and gourmet grocers' shelves with their popular, versatile line of triple-duty marinade, grilling, and barbecue sauces. My favorite with barbecue is the sweet and tangy Honey Mustard. Brown mustard seeds add flavor and texture in the honey-sweetened base blended with Dijon mustard and other seasonings. It's good as a finishing or dipping sauce with chicken and pork. Honey Teriyaki works best as a marinade or stir-fry sauce, with its tangy, garlic-laced thin soy sauce base. The Sweet 'n' Sour Grilling Sauce carries a flavorful tangy sweetness that is great on chicken breast and pork ribs. Mesquite is a good cowboy sauce, lending a tangy, spicy, smoky complement to beef brisket. Lemon Pepper is delicious on grilled pork chops or chicken breasts, a tangy lemon flavor complement. Spices add texture to the smooth sauce base, which includes buttermilk.

MAULL'S BARBECUE SAUCE
ST. LOUIS, MISSOURI

Some call Maull's the traditional barbecue sauce of Missouri. Others give it a more local accolade: the official favorite of St. Louis. Maull's is a ketchupy nectar that has slathered the ribs, burgers, brats, and hot dogs of the people of St. Louis for over seventy years. The original flavor base of tomato ketchup with a bite of pepper, vinegar tanginess, and a hint of secret spices is augmented with eight variations—Smoky, Kansas City Style, Sweet-N-Smoky, Jalapeño, Onion Bits, Sweet-N-Mild, Beer Flavor, and Lite. Legions of Maull's fans live by the product slogan: "Don't baste your barbecue. Maull it!"

OKLAHOMA JOE'S BARBECUE SAUCE
NEW BRAUNFELS, TEXAS

Joe Don Davidson knows the art and sport of barbecue. After winning many cooking contests, Joe decided to put his sauce on the market in 1993. That year, shortly after the sauce went into production, it won Best Barbecue Sauce on the Planet at the American Royal International Barbecue Sauce Contest—excelling among almost 400 other competitors. There's nothing fancy about the label or the sauce. Although the ingredients are in the mainstream of traditional tomato-based sauces, the way it's put together is exceptional. Oklahoma Joe's Barbecue Sauce is easy on the tongue, with a sweet combination of tomato ketchup, Worcestershire sauce, black pepper, and spices that makes a perfect complement to pork, beef, poultry, fish, grilled vegetables, and much more.

OLD AUBRY
BARBECUE SAUCE
GARDNER, KANSAS

Ward Billings sat with at least 800 barbecue pitmasters and saucemasters, on folding chairs, hay bales, and tarmac, waiting for the results of the American Royal International Barbecue Sauce Contest and the American Royal Barbecue competition. He had entered Old Aubry in the sauce contest on a whim. Given the size of the contest, with over 300 competitors, he had no idea how Old Aubry would impress the judges. When the late Buck Buchanan, honorary chair of the sauce contest, announced that Old Aubry had won Best Barbecue Sauce on the Planet, Ward went into orbit. Old Aubry was the house sauce at the former Aubry Inn in Stillwell, Kansas, where Ward worked as chef. Now Old Aubry is owned and produced by Ward Billings. Thick, spicy, tomato-based and rich in molasses, Old Aubry isn't just another barbecue sauce. The spicy-sweet bite from peppers is eased with a refreshing hint of island spices, such as allspice or cloves. Old Aubry will make your ribs, pork, brisket, and chicken taste better. Use as a finishing or dipping sauce, or as Ward suggests, thin it with beer or bourbon for use as a marinade or mopping sauce.

OLD FORT GOURMET
BAR-B-Q SAUCE
FORT SCOTT, KANSAS

Old Fort's regionally famous, award-winning flavor is beginning to catch national attention. Fort Scott, Kansas, where Old Fort is made, sprang up in frontier days near a Western outpost army fort. Now the fort is a tourist attraction, and the town has diversified into agribusiness, education, and technology-related industries. Ken Lunt, a local power and light company executive, is the keeper of the Old Fort recipe, which Mr. Lunt's ancestors developed almost a hundred years ago. When you open an Old Fort bottle, the smoky tomato bouquet prepares you to like it. The sweet, full-bodied smoky flavor with a gentle peppery finish is superb on barbecued beef brisket, pork ribs, pork shoulder, and chicken. It also livens up a baked bean casserole or a meat loaf. Unique among barbecue sauces, Old Fort is made by nuns. All profits help pay medical bills of uninsured or underinsured patients at Fort Scott's Mercy Hospital.

THE ORIGINAL PEPPER CREEK FARMS BARBECUE SAUCE

LAWTON, OKLAHOMA

Dressed in a red bandana and a red or black cowboy hat, Pepper Creek Farms Barbecue Sauce makes no bones about appealing to the cowboy in you. You will not be disappointed by this sauce. The initial burst of tangy, tongue-tingling sweet tomato flavor is quickly followed by a gentle bite of hot pepper and a hint of mesquite smoke from a cowboy campfire. The appearance is so smooth that it's a refreshing surprise to find tiny bits of fresh garlic and onion in an otherwise totally blended serenade.

RITA ANN BARBEQUE SAUCE

KANSAS CITY, MISSOURI

You can taste over ninety years of Kansas City barbecue history in Rita Ann Barbeque Sauce. Family members who descend from brothers Martin and Julius Blender haven't reached consensus on whether Rita Ann tastes like the "real" sauce from the original Blender's Barbecue Restaurant of the early 1900s, but all agree that the original was much hotter. Fortunately for us, Rita Ann Shapiro, granddaughter of Martin Blender, the pitmaster at Blender's, spent a lot of time trying to duplicate the recipe. It doesn't matter if it's the original Blender's. It matters that it's good. Rita Ann is a splendid, fresh-tasting tomato-based sauce, gently spiced, sweet, slightly peppery, with a hint of celery. It will make your barbecue taste better. Use it as a dipping sauce and in baked beans.

ROADHOUSE BAR-B-QUE SAUCE

DES PLAINES, ILLINOIS

I've been a Roadhouse fan since my first bite in 1992. The tangy-sweet flavor is delivered in a tomato base laced with vinegar, pineapple, and raisins. The base flavor is enhanced with a hint of smoke and secret spices.

Fiery eaters should get Roadhouse Hot & Spicy. When it slaps your tongue, your tongue will beg for more. Roadhouse also makes an excellent Bar-B-Que Salsa, which adds a Southwestern accent to the signature flavor and chunky texture of Roadhouse. Roadhouse has a consistent record of winning ribbons in prestigious sauce and cooking contests. Company founder Jeff Sanders developed this product from an old family recipe. Use Roadhouse on all grilled and barbecued foods and try it with other foods—as a spread with cream cheese, a great addition to baked beans, or as an egg-roll topper.

ROBERT ROTHSCHILD STOCKYARD BARBECUE SAUCE

URBANA, OHIO

The eight-ounce faceted glass jar with green and gold labeling is stamped "Robert Rothschild," a name which has become famous for gourmet foods and condiments. Stockyard Barbecue Sauce lives up to the Rothschild reputation. The sweet, thick, chunky tomato base is perfectly balanced with a touch of tanginess and a chile pepper finish hinting of chocolate. It works well as a finishing and dipping sauce with the full spectrum of barbecued and grilled meats. I like it best with barbecued beef brisket.

ROSCOE'S BARBEQUE SAUCE

ROCHESTER, MINNESOTA

When life gave him a vintage A&W Root Beer stand, Steven "Roscoe" Ross made root beer and ribs. Unemployed and low on cash, Roscoe convinced the owner of a closed root beer stand in Rochester, Minnesota, to give him the equipment in the stand to use as collateral for a loan to buy the stand. The deal worked, and the result was the birth of a shining star in the barbecue universe. Steve's sauce recipe evolved from one given to him by Gail McFarland, a former co-worker at a steak house, who gave him her mother's recipe. An exclusive flavor feature of Roscoe's is honey from happy bees at the B & B Honey Farm, at the end of a dead-end road in a beautiful Minnesota river valley. Roscoe's award-winning, tangy, sweet, spicy flavor is excellent on barbecued pork ribs, pig sandwiches, chicken, and beef. Heat the sauce for maximum taste. "Good barbecue," says Roscoe, "is a marriage between the sauce and the meat. It is not one or the other." Try some Roscoe's on your ribs, and you'll see what he means.

ROUTE 66 BARBECUE SAUCE
BRISTOW, OKLAHOMA

Route 66 Barbecue Sauce comes in a white plastic jug, shaped like an antifreeze container. Inside the jug is a smooth, burnt-orange sauce with hints of black pepper flakes. It is another sweet tomato-based sauce, but Route 66 isn't just another barbecue sauce. It is mainstream enough to taste familiar, but its spicy, sweet, tangy flavors are different enough to command your attention and your loyalty, on or off the road.

SAGAWA'S POLYNESIAN BBQ SAUCE
TUALATIN, OREGON

If island gods eat barbecue, Sagawa's Polynesian BBQ Sauce is always on the table. Dr. Jim Sagawa, a dentist from Hawaii, founded Sagawa's Savory Sauces in Tualatin, Oregon, in 1983. His sauce was tested over twenty-five years of entertaining friends and family before he put it on the market. Soy sauce, pineapple juice, and toasted sesame oil are the signature flavors. They are blended to smooth perfection with sugars, ginger, secret spices, and some familiar ingredients such as vinegar, onion, and peppers. My favorite use of Sagawa's is as a dipping sauce with pork or chicken. It is also excellent as a stir-fry sauce.

SILVER DOLLAR CITY ORIGINAL RECIPE BARBECUE SAUCE

BRANSON, MISSOURI

From the Ozark hills of Missouri, which have boomed as a tourist attraction in recent years, Silver Dollar City Original Recipe Barbecue Sauce is a good example of the basic sweet, smooth, tomato-based barbecue sauce with a touch of hickory smoke that is so popular in Middle America. Used in moderation, this sauce is terrific with barbecued pork ribs, beef brisket, chicken, lamb, and duck. Use it also as a flavorful substitute for ketchup on fried potatoes or omelettes. Variations of the Original Recipe are Ozark, Sweet & Mild, All-Purpose, and Tangy.

SIR CHARLES BAR-B-QUE SAUCE

PHOENIX, ARIZONA

Although of Texas heritage, this sauce is made in Arizona. It has the orange hue of many Florida sauces. The flavor of Sir Charles, however, resists regional comparison. This smooth-textured pit sauce carries a touch of sweetness, with herbal accents, compatible with beef, chicken, and pork. Use it warm as a dipping sauce or finishing sauce to bring out the full flavor. Charles Taylor, of Phoenix, developed this sauce from a recipe handed down to him from his great-great grandfather, George Williams. Mr. Williams developed the recipe while working as a cook on a large Texas ranch many years ago. He would be proud that his great-great grandson is continuing the legacy of his sauce. Available in original and hot styles.

SONNY BRYAN'S SMOKE-HOUSE BBQ SAUCE

DALLAS, TEXAS

Fortunately for you and me, Sonny Bryan sold his smokehouse before he died. Otherwise the red-haired Dallas legend's barbecue would be talked about in the past tense, as in, "You shoulda been there." Fortunately, it's still there, and "you oughta go." Regardless of which location you choose—Sonny's original, or the several new locations around town—you'll never forget your first time at Sonny's. Sonny Bryan's Smokehouse BBQ Sauce is smoky, Texas red, smooth, semisweet, and tangy, with a gentle chile pepper afterburn. Sonny served it warm, and so should you.

SOUTHERN RAY'S SOUTHERN STYLE BARBECUE SAUCE

MIAMI BEACH, FLORIDA

Southern Ray Goodstone puts his name on the label and his remarkable culinary talents into each jar of Southern Ray Barbecue Sauce. Southern Style is the flagship sauce of the Southern Ray fleet. Ray enhances its sweet tomato base with lime juice, Worcestershire sauce, fresh garlic, secret spices, and an herbal finish. Roasted Garlic & Ginger is a slight variation from Southern Style with added sweetness and zest from small, flavorful chunks of roasted garlic and ginger. Smoky Garlic & Ginger adds refreshing hickory smoke flavor to fresh garlic and ginger in a thicker variation of Southern Style. Southern Ray's Honey & Orange is a dramatic departure from Southern style tomato-based sauces: Orange and naturally brewed soy sauce kisses and balances the rich sweetness of pure honey.  Southern Ray's sauces make any ordinary barbecue extraordinary. They are versatile enough to work as all-purpose sauces in vegetable dishes, stir-fry, dips, soups, and meat loaf.

Ray makes an excellent Maple Teriyaki and a fat-free Apple & Wine Marinade. For palates that demand fire, Ray makes an excellent Three Pepper Sauce fired from hot cherry, jalapeño, and cayenne peppers, with an herbal finish. His Island Pepper is the fiery companion to Honey & Orange. It delivers sensual honey-and-orange sweetness, finished with a fiery jalapeño and scotch bonnet pepper blast.

SOUTHERN ROADHOUSE BARBECUE SAUCE
OAKLAND, CALIFORNIA

The nostalgic label may attract your interest, but the old-fashioned Southern flavors will bring you back for more. Southern Roadhouse contains an eclectic variety of popular Southern barbecue complements. Pepper, spices, red wine vinegar, molasses and other natural sweeteners, hickory smoke, onion, and garlic are masterfully blended in a thick tomato base. The result is a tangy sweet sauce with a strong, spicy finish. It goes well with all of your favorite barbecued meats. Use it as a finishing sauce or a dipping sauce.

SPAGHETTI WESTERN HOT STUFF BARBECUE
TESUQUE, NEW MEXICO

I like a sauce with a good sense of humor. Julie of New Mexico lets her humor shine with Spaghetti Western Hot Stuff Barbecue sauces. The name is slang for low-budget Western movies filmed in Italy years ago. Julie makes the sauce in New Mexico, where real cowboys and cowgirls have made a living for many years. Since Spaghetti Western sauces are "handmade in small batches," they are low-budget productions compared to the giants in the industry. The quality, however, is never low. The white label sauce, when used as a dipping sauce, has the wholesome, delicate, comforting flavor of tomato spiced with chile peppers. The red label sauce delivers a more robust, smoky flavor, with a strong chile pepper finish. When heated or used as a finishing sauce, the New Mexico-grown chiles will bite a little bit more, but not on the fiery side.

SPOTTED BULL BBQ SAUCE
COLUMBUS, KANSAS

Originally known as "Spotted Cow," this delicious barbecue sauce made by Jim and Ruth Hale in Columbus, Kansas, changed genders after a trademark search. Spotted Bull's thick tomato base is brown-sugar sweet, chunky, slightly smoky, and wholesome. It is versatile enough to complement a variety of barbecue and nonbarbecue foods, but goes especially well with barbecued beef brisket and in baked beans. My favorite variety is Blazing Bull, the hot version of Spotted Bull. It is the same sauce with a double measure of black and red pepper, but it won't set your mouth on fire. In addition to complementing barbecued and grilled foods, Spotted Bull sauces are the perfect dipping sauces for battered and deep-fried Rocky Mountain oysters.

STATIC'S BARBECUE SAUCE
BREAUX BRIDGE, LOUISIANA

The All Cajun Food Company, creator of Static's Sweet & Spicy Barbecue Sauce and Static's Chunky Onion Barbecue Sauce, has a motto: "It's time to shake things up a bit." With their barbecue sauces and an acclaimed line of other sauces and seasonings, All Cajun gives you the power to shake things up and get out of a culinary rut. Static's Sweet & Spicy is a fusion of a familiar sweet tomato-based sauce with a refreshing spicy pepper and Cajun herbal finish. Chunky Onion adds the texture of chopped onions to the smooth Sweet & Spicy blend. Keep both on hand. I like to use Sweet & Spicy as a finishing sauce and Chunky Onion for presentation on meat, or on the side for dipping.

STEEL'S ROCKY MOUNTAIN BARBEQUE SAUCE

BRIDGEPORT, PENNSYLVANIA

Although this sauce is made in Pennsylvania, Betty Jo Steel took her birthplace near the Montana Rockies as the inspiration for the name of Steel's Rocky Mountain Barbeque Sauce. This sauce is an excellent choice when you're entertaining an intergenerational backyard gathering at the grill or with outdoor campfire cooking. The mild, ketchupy flavor will complement backyard burgers, grilled fish, chicken, pork ribs, and vegetables. It's also good on fried potatoes, deep-fried rocky mountain oysters, pig fries, and really great on grilled shrimp. The smooth texture clings well to food, making Steel's versatile as a marinade or dip. The sauce is also Kosher and "may be useful for diabetics on the advice of a health professional."

STONEWALL KITCHEN MAPLE "CHIPOLTE" GRILLE SAUCE

YORK, MAINE

Stonewall Kitchen Maple Chipolte Grille Sauce is a creative fusion of maple sweet Northeastern and spicy Southwestern flavors. The first bite picks you up with a comforting sweetness reminiscent of apple pie. Gradually the minced chives, garlic, onion, chile powder, and other spices add accent. A gentle bite from chipotle gives this sauce a Southwestern finish. Although called a grill sauce, Stonewall Grille Sauce is excellent as a barbecue dipping sauce with all varieties of barbecue meat or grilled meats and vegetables. Maple Chipolte Grille Sauce includes some ingredients traditional to tomato-based sauces, but the flavor of this award-winning sauce is unlike any other.

SYLVIA'S RESTAURANT QUEEN OF SOUL FOOD ORIGINAL SAUCE

NEW YORK, NEW YORK

Her trademark title is "Queen of Soul Food." Sylvia Woods opened her first restaurant in New York City's Harlem over thirty years ago. Her cuisine is rooted in the foods she learned to cook from her mother, as a child in South Carolina. Sylvia's is an outstanding all-purpose barbecue finishing or dipping sauce for chicken, pork ribs, beef brisket, grilled burgers, or baked foods such as meat loaf. The sweet, orange-red, smooth tomato base of the sauce is laced with small chunks of onion, pepper, and celery, giving it an excellent fresh-tasting finish. The Hot & Sassy is a gentle hot; you can add Sylvia's own Kicking Hot Hot Sauce, or another of your favorites for extra fire.

TENNESSEE MASTERPIECE GOURMET BARBECUE SAUCE

RIDGETOP, TENNESSEE

It takes courage to call your sauce a masterpiece and to name it after a state that is famous for barbecue. Ron Boyle has the courage, and Tennessee Masterpiece Gourmet Barbecue Sauce lives up to its name. Smooth and dark in a tomato base, this sauce's sweet, spicy flavor finishes with a gentle hit from chile peppers. It's outstanding as a finishing and dipping sauce with all of your favorite foods from the pit or grill.

TENNESSEE TUCKER'S TANTALIZING RIB SAUCE

NASHVILLE, TENNESSEE

Ronald Tucker is religious about sauce. A few years ago, while at home from his job at the Ford Glass Plant in Nashville, Ronald was so caught up in the desire to make a fantastic sauce for his ribs, chicken, and pork shoulder that he prayed for divine guidance. The result is Tennessee Tucker's Tantalizing Rib Sauce. Ronald says his sauce is "the best you'll get this side of Heaven." With sauce this good, however, Heaven can wait. Tennessee Tucker's mild sauce is a complex blend of tangy, sweet, and power-packed spices that earn the designation "tantalizing." The mild version is spicy enough to be considered hot to pepper-sensitive palates. The hot version delivers the same punch as the mild with a slow, gentle, burn. Both sauces are excellent finishing or dipping sauces with ribs, shoulder, and chicken.

TORTUGA RUM BAR-B-QUE SAUCE

GEORGE TOWN, GRAND CAYMAN ISLAND, B.W.I.

The simulated parchment label features pirate ships and is bordered in ship rope. The sauce features sugar and rum. Besides sugar and rum, the thick tomato base has enough vinegar to lend a slight tanginess, with a smoky, spicy finish. Use Tortuga Rum Bar-B-Que Sauce during the last five minutes of grilling, the last fifteen minutes of barbecuing, and as an exceptional dipping sauce with all barbecued meats.

TOUCH OF SOUTH ALL-PURPOSE BARBEQUE SAUCE

INGLEWOOD, CALIFORNIA

When you try Touch of South All Purpose Barbeque Sauce, you'll understand why it has been a success for more than twenty years. Due to the enormous local popularity of their sauce, Michael Beatty, a friend of Lillian and Paul Kidd, convinced them to put it on the market in 1976. Touch of South's complex blend of sixteen secret spices in a grainy tomato base with sugar, vinegar, lemon juice, and hickory smoke lends a savory, sweet, smoky complement to your barbecued or ovenbaked meats. Besides Southern spices, there's a hint of Southwestern chile flavors. Touch of South is great as a finishing and dipping sauce on all barbecued meats, and in beans, chili, and a variety of other foods.

TR'S GREAT AMERICAN BARBECUE SAUCE

WILLISTON PARK, NEW YORK

Bearing the initials of America's twenty-sixth president, this rich, hearty, honey-sweetened tomato-based sauce with a hint of mesquite smoke is the only one I've found that is named after a U.S. president. Theodore Roosevelt left a bold imprint on history as cowboy, assistant secretary of the navy, Rough Rider media-savvy president, and Bull Moose candidate. He also sprinkled some sugar on his trail of fame. TR's Honey Mesquite pays tribute to the sweet, soft-speaking, side of Teddy.

Fiery feeders can get a hit from Teddy's big stick by adding habañero sauce, or switching to TR's Great American Buffalo Wing Sauce—a vinegar and cayenne pepper-based sauce that will increase in spiciness when heated.

VERMONT GOLD GRILLING AND ROASTING SAUCE

BRATTLEBORO, VERMONT

When you're looking for fantastic gourmet sauce that goes beyond traditional barbecue sauce flavors, Vermont Gold Grilling and Roasting Sauce is the perfect find. Sesame Garlic, my favorite, is maple syrup sweet, with a touch of citrus fruit tanginess and the unbeatable combination of tamari, toasted sesame oil, garlic, and other seasonings. Put it on grilled pork loin, barbecued pork shoulder, chicken, or seafood. Cranberry Ginger delivers cranberry and ginger root tanginess balanced with maple syrup sweetness. Try it with barbecued chicken, turkey, or ham. Mandarin Orange complements chicken or fish, especially salmon, with the refreshing flavors of orange, maple syrup, olive oil, and herbs.

WHISKY BASIN WHISKY FLAVORED BARBEQUE SAUCE WITH JALAPEÑO PEPPERS

SHAWNEE MISSION, KANSAS

The award-winning Whisky Basin package is an attention grabber. Shaped like a whisky bottle and attractively labeled with red product script on a black background and a cattle drive scene à la Frederic Remington, the bottle almost shouts at you from the shelf, "I'm different. Pick me up!" The Whisky Basin difference goes beyond the bottle and the label. Whisky Basin is purported to be the invention of a Kansas City cook and some Southern moonshiners on a cattle drive to Montana. They liked a place called "Whisky Basin" so well that they decided to keep the cattle and stay. The Southerners set up a still to begin whisky production, while the Kansas City cook began developing a barbecue sauce. With so much cattle to barbecue, you've got to have sauce. Whisky Basin's artful blend of puréed tomatoes, brown sugar, slightly chunky onion, garlic, whiskey flavor, a gentle bite of jalapeño pepper, and a hint of secret spices brings out the best in beef brisket, chicken, ribs, and a variety of nonbarbecue foods. Try this sauce on hot dogs, fried potatoes, scrambled eggs, or fajitas. It will earn a permanent place in your private stock for all occasions. Best when heated.

WILLINGHAM'S SWEET & SASSY WHAM SAUCE

MEMPHIS, TENNESSEE

I call John Willingham the Leonardo da Vinci of Barbecue. He is inventive, artistic, passionate about excellence, and quick-witted. John's perfect sense of timing, an eye for presentation, and his magic touch with mops, cleavers, and seasonings. When you're in the mood for sweet and spicy, but not hot, Willingham's Sweet & Sassy Wham Sauce is fantastic. The blend of molasses, sugar, chocolate, and John Willingham's secret spices in a tomato base make this sauce stand above the crowd. John makes a variety of other sauces. Although the splendid Original Hot was the first hot sauce to win Best on the Planet at the American Royal (1992), Cajun Hot is my favorite. The complex blend of spices in a thick, tangy, tomato base and spicy hot Cajun flavor finish is perfect for people who like moderate fire. John's For Big Kids Only Hot wastes no time flaming through the tangy, spicy tomato base. You can pump up the intensity by adding Wham Hot Stuff dry seasonings.

WINSLOW'S KANSAS CITY STYLE ORIGINAL RECIPE BBQ SAUCE

KANSAS CITY, MISSOURI

Kansas City locals called the late Don Winslow the "Sultan of Smoke." The Sultan and his family established Winslow's City Market Smokehouse in 1971. Fortunately the Winslow quelinary tradition continues in this historic location. The new label on the sauce features a pink pig face on the mild sauce and a red pig face with devilish horns on the "wild." The wild is called River Quay Red Spicy BBQ Sauce and is a recent addition at Winslow's. Both tomato-based sauces give a tangy, spicy, sweet complement to barbecued beef, chicken, and pork. River Quay Red is slightly hotter than original recipe.

ZABE AND ZOLIE'S FAMOUS KANSAS CITY BBQ SAUCE

KANSAS CITY, MISSOURI

Bob "Zabe" Zaban developed this award-winning sauce over thirty years ago. When he partnered with Zolie Gilgus to enter the 1986 Great Lenexa Bar-B-Que Battle, they emerged as the Kansas grand champions. They have been winning awards, catering barbecue, and selling sauce ever since. Zabe and Zolie's lands on the familiar sweet, tomato-based side of the Kansas City barbecue palate. Their spices, however, are a blend of unique and traditional Kansas City flavors. A hint of anise boosts Zabe and Zolie's above the crowd and into the winner's circle. This sauce is great as a finishing and dipping sauce with pork, poultry, beef, and fish. They also make a hot version of the sauce and a dry rub that won Best on the Planet in 1997.

ZIM'S ORIGINAL BARBECUE SAUCE
CASTLE ROCK, COLORADO

Although they now make Zim's in Colorado, its birthplace is Cedar Rapids, Iowa, where its originator, Kermit Zimmerman (Zim), still lives and now sells his sauce in area grocery stores. Zim developed this sauce for his restaurant in the early 1970s. Since then Zim's Original Barbecue Sauce has been a popular take-home sauce. Zim's Family Foods was created in 1992 and operates as a contract packager for other sauces, plus a catering, food concessions, and takeout lunch business. Zim's Original is a smooth, sweet tomato-based sauce enhanced with a gentle touch of Worcestershire sauce, mustard, garlic, onion, oregano, chile powder, and pepper. It makes your mouth feel mellow and coaxes your meat from good to excellent. The hotter version, Zim's Hot Pepper, varies slightly from the original but still delivers a smooth flavor with kicks from red pepper and cayenne pepper.

TANGY
SAUCES

JIM BEAM KENTUCKY BOURBON BARBEQUE SAUCE
ATLANTA, GEORGIA

Attractively packaged with a Jim Beam Kentucky Bourbon label, this peppery, slightly tangy sauce in a tomato base is sure to satisfy more than just bourbon fans in its reach for satisfied customers. Vinegar, citrus juices, a touch of molasses, a gentle bite from peppers, and a touch of Kentucky bourbon is the signature flavor combo. Smooth, with tiny chunks of onion and pineapple, Jim Beam Kentucky Bourbon Barbeque Sauce will stick to your ribs, chicken, and brisket. It's also recommended for a delicious flavor enhancer in your meat loaf.

BILLY BONES B.B.Q. SAUCE
SANFORD, MICHIGAN

William E. "Billy Bones" Wall has burned more apple trees than Johnny Appleseed ever planted. Billy doesn't waste the wood, though, and he never takes a tree before its time. After you've tasted what Billy can do with apple wood smoke and pork ribs, you'll wonder why anyone bothers with any other wood for barbecue. Add a dash of Billy Bones B.B.Q. Sauce to your ribs, and you'll want to move as close to Billy's pit in Sanford, Michigan, as possible. Fortunately, many rib eaters get to meet Billy and eat his ribs at rib cookoffs around the country. If Michigan and ribfests are beyond your reach, you can still get a taste of Billy Bones barbecue. Get a bottle of Billy's sauce, smoke your ribs with apple wood, and enjoy a taste of heaven on earth. Billy's tomato-based sauce has a hint of sweetness and a hint of smoke, but the signature is a vinegar tanginess and a bite of black pepper. Billy Bones B.B.Q. Sauce is great as a dipping sauce with a variety of barbecued meats and grilled vegetables, and it works even better when applied to ribs five minutes before serving time. You and your guests will devour all but the bones. Maybe that's how Billy got his name.

BRAZOS 2-POT
BAR-B-QUE SAUCE
BRYAN, TEXAS

When you pour some Brazos 2-Pot Bar-B-Que Sauce on your tender, smoky, barbecue beef brisket and take a bite, you'll get an idea of how Brazos County, Texas, became the brisket capital of the world. Brazos is not sweet, and it is not bodaciously spicy; it is tangy, with savory overtones. The smooth tomato base, in combination with Worcestershire sauce, vinegar, lemon juice, and secret spices known only to Craig Conlee, his father, and his uncle, treats your brisket with the respect it deserves. The Conlees call Brazos "2-Pot" because it starts with part of the ingredients in one simmering pot and the other part in another. Just when the flavors in each pot peak, the two are combined. Brazos also makes a 2-Pot Mesquite Bar-B-Que Sauce, similar in flavor to the original, with a smoky finish. I prefer the original. Brazos adds an exceptional complement to barbecued ribs and chicken too.

ARTHUR BRYANT'S ORIGINAL
BARBEQUE SAUCE
KANSAS CITY, MISSOURI

When Mr. Bryant was alive, he corked the big glass water bottles filled with aging sauce behind the front windows of his world-famous "greasehouse." Today the sauce still ages up front, but crumpled aluminum foil has replaced the corks. Arthur Bryant's is a breed apart from what most people expect in a barbecue sauce—grainy, with a cumin-dominant curry flavor accented with vinegar, a hint of tomato, and a kiss of smoke flavor from the barbecue pit. An Arthur Bryant beef sandwich with fries is not complete without this sauce. It is also outstanding on pork, chicken, and on the fries. Bryant's sauce is an acquired taste that will become a lifelong favorite. There are people who can't get a good night's sleep without the comforting knowledge that they have stashed a bottle of Arthur Bryant's in the cupboard. You may end up craving it in the middle of the night.

BUBBA BRAND
BUBBA Q SAUCE
CHARLESTON, SOUTH CAROLINA

Southern Bubbas abound in many shapes and sizes. The one silhouetted on this label symbolizes "Everybubba." He sits with his arms folded in front, sauce bottle on the table, wearing a gimme cap. He listens intently to the Bubba on his right. These twin, or cloned, Bubbas make a perfect symbol for a sauce that captures the essence of a way of life. The touch of sweetness from molasses and sugarcane juice is nudged by tangy cider vinegar accented with tomato and spices. Bubba Brand is an excellent basting and finishing sauce on pork and chicken—a great gift sauce too.

BUCKAROO TANGY APPLE
BAR-B-QUE SAUCE
BARTLESVILLE, OKLAHOMA

Inspired by traditional Texas and Oklahoma cowboy campfire cooking, Buckaroo Tangy Apple Bar-B-Que Sauce balances tangy apple sauce with tomato ketchup to enhance a subtle mix of secret spices. Worcestershire sauce and lemon juice kick in for additional tang. Buckaroo is best when served warm as a dipping sauce or brushed on meat the last ten minutes of cooking. It complements barbecued beef, pork, chicken, and sausage. For a sweeter, spicier complement, try Cowcamp Meat Sauce. Both are made by a Southwestern specialty foods corporation called Best of the West.

CACTUS WILLY'S GREEN CHILE AND CILANTRO BBQ SAUCE

GLENDALE, ARIZONA

At fist glance this sauce may seem an odd mix, but after a taste, it will make perfect sense. Mild green chile peppers puréed with finely minced cilantro give this suce a smooth, traditional texture but an unusually tangy taste. The sauce is tomato based, with some of the expected ingredients such as molasses and vinegar. Cactus Willy's is excellent on grilled chicken, and for something different, try using it in place of salsa on baked nachos.

CAFE TEQUILA

SAN FRANCISCO, CALIFORNIA

The first thing that strikes you about this sauce is its very distinctive bottle. I cannot recall any other sauce, or any product, that comes in such a bottle shape. While the package certainly is a show stopper, the sauce will also grab your attention. One word describes the flavor: intense! Some sweet, some savory, a bit of heat, blended masterfully into a perfect consistency that makes Cafe Tequila an ideal finishing sauce. A little bit goes a long way, so it works well brushed on in a thin layer, rather than slathering it. While this sauce is fine with all types of meats and poultry, my favorite use is brushed lightly over grilled salmon.

CALHOUN'S TASTE OF TENNESSEE ALL NATURAL BAR-B-QUE SAUCE

KNOXVILLE, TENNESSEE

Since owner Michael Chase won Best Ribs in America at the National Rib Cookoff in Cleveland, Ohio, thousands of customers have taken well-deserved notice of his sauce and his barbecue. Less vinegar and more vegetable oil makes Calhoun's

tomato-based sauce differ from many other Tennessee sauces, but the traditional "taste of Tennessee" comes through in this rich, full-bodied
sauce with a taste of vinegar and a pepper accent
reminiscent of French dressing. Shake it well to
mix the soybean oil with the other ingredients.

CAROLINA CUPBOARD
CHAPEL HILL, NORTH CAROLINA

If there is one region of the United States that is known for
diverse tastes for barbecue sauces, it is the Carolinas. The
folks down there generally go for pork as their barbecue meat
of choice, but that's where any similarities end. Some like
their barbecue with a thin sauce of vinegar and chile peppers,
some with a mustard sauce, and others with a thick tomato-
based sauce sweetened with molasses and brown sugar. Carolina Cupboard produces an Eastern North Carolina Style
Sauce composed of a basic blend of cider vinegar and brown
sugar, with some chile pepper and spices. Don't let the red-
dish color fool you. This is a tomato-free sauce. This sauce is
to be used more for splashing on meat after its been grilled
or barbecued, but it also works quite well as a marinade. It's
a simple sauce with a crisp flavor and a bit of tang ending with
a touch of heat.

To the west, they like their barbeque sauce with some sweetness to it. Carolina Cupboard's Western North Carolina Style
Sauce delivers a rich, sweet, but not too sweet taste—a nice
blend of the ketchup, molasses, cider vinegar, Worcestershire
sauce, brown sugar, and a dash of salt and spices. It's perfect
for slow cooking and frequent basting. Keep a bowl
nearby for dipping too. Defining barbecue allegiance in
this part of the country can be confusing, whether its
Western North Carolina, Eastern North Carolina,
Eastern South Carolina, Western South Carolina,
Northern South Carolina, or Southern North
Carolina, but the barbecue here will keep your
compass spinning. Just remember, they do know
barbecue in the Carolinas, and its ALL good!

CHILE TODAY HOT TAMALE SMOKY CHIPOTLE BARBEQUE SAUCE

EAST HANOVER, NEW JERSEY

The chipotle pepper has been showing up in a variety of food products these days. While many sauces burn your taste buds with a variety of fiery peppers, some, such as this sauce, have used the chipotle to create a very tasty and tangy way to add some zip to barbecue sauce. The chipotle is actually a jalapeño pepper that has been smoked, which reduces a lot of the heat but adds a terrific flavor note to the barbecue.

This is the first venture into barbecue sauce for Chile Today Hot Tamale, who have made their name through their line of exotic, premium dried chile peppers and snack foods. This sauce is expertly blended, with the smoky flavor of the pepper balanced with the dark sweetness of molasses. The addition of a microbrew ale, minced onion, and mustard flour help give this sauce a thick texture that would hold up well as a finishing sauce and as a dipping sauce.

COTTONFIELDS BBQ WHITE SAUCE

MADISON, ALABAMA

This sauce is white with black specks—like a clear glass jar full of puréed cotton bolls. The resemblance to puréed cotton stops at appearance. Born of the Alabama affection for white sauce, Cottonfields will make you rethink how you like your chicken. The smooth, thick texture holds well to the meat, and the spices and vinegar take the flavor beyond ordinary mayonnaise. This sauce is great as a finishing or dipping sauce for grilled chicken, pork chops, seafood, and freshwater fish, especially catfish—and also perfect as a potato salad or coleslaw dressing.

COUCH'S ORIGINAL SAUCE
JONESBORO, ARKANSAS

Couch's makes one sauce, one variety, and as they say in Jonesboro, "Couch's is nobody's cousin." Couch's Corner Bar-B-Q has been in business for twenty-five years, and it is such a popular local pork palace that it seems like it's been there forever. Good cooking with good sauce keeps people coming back. Couch's sauce is a tart and peppery blend of vinegar, tomato, and secret spices. It's an excellent finishing or dipping sauce with barbecued meats and also great in barbecue beans. Eating at Couch's is worth a trip to Jonesboro, but if you can't make the trip, the sauce is available by the case.

CRAIG'S ORIGINAL BARBECUE SAUCE
BRINKLEY, ARKANSAS

A creation of barbecue expert Lawrence Craig, Craig's Original Barbecue Sauce is one of the many unsung treasures of Arkansas. The bottle is a departure from the traditional sauce jug, and the contents depart from most sauces you'll find in supermarkets today. When poured and tasted, Craig's steps even further from the mainstream. Wow! This special blend of citrus, vinegar, peppers, paprika, and other spices is a breed of its own, with a thin, vinegary tanginess and a peppery citrus finish. It's an outstanding complement to chicken, pork ribs, and any other part of a barbecued hog. Craig's is available in mild, medium hot, or hot. Sample all three to find your comfort zone.

CRAZY JERRY'S SWINE WINE
ROSWELL, GEORGIA

Although labeled as a basting sauce, Crazy Jerry's "Hawg Heaven (Mild)" Swine Wine is a perfect grabber for those days when sweet just won't do it. The mustard base, fused with pepper, vinegar, lemon juice, and secret spices, is tangy and just on the edge of pleasantly sour. It's fantastic on pork and chicken.

Crazy Jerry's Alotta Bull tomato-based finishing and dipping sauces come in sMOOth mild and Torrid Toro hot. Both are thick, chunky, and laced with concentrated lemon juice and savory spices. Naturally, these are for your beef.

DIXIE TRAIL FARMS BBQ SAUCE
CARY, NORTH CAROLINA

A 1920s era photo of a boy named Little Sam sitting atop a huge hog named Bacon is the centerpiece for the Dixie Trail Farms label. The sauce is a daring combination of the two barbecue sauce bases that prevail in North Carolina, vinegar and tomato. Battles still rage today over which base is best. Dixie Trail Farms boldly uses both. Few will argue that the hybrid doesn't work. Shake it well and sprinkle it on your barbecue. Apple cider vinegar dominates the tomato, but together the vinegar and tomato give an excellent balance to the peppers and other spices. Dixie Trail Farms excels as a hog sauce for finishing and for sprinkling on chopped or pulled pork. It's available in mild and hot, but the hot is only slightly hotter than the mild.

EATON'S ORIGINAL JERK BARBEQUE SAUCE
KINGSTON, JAMAICA

The traditional formula for Jamaican jerk more closely resembles a paste than a sauce and does not contain any tomato. At first look Eaton's Original may seem a barbecue sauce gone awry, but after tasting grilled chicken basted with this sauce you'll change your tune. This thick tomato-based sauce eschews the usual burning heat of the traditional jerk rubs for a very pleasant hint of heat, with some unexpected flavor from scallions and pimento. It works well as a finishing baste and as a dipping sauce for chicken, beef, and pork of all varieties, particularly baby back ribs.

ELLA'S ULTIMATE BARBECUE SAUCE
SAVANNAH, GEORGIA

Ella's looks like the kind of sauce you'd expect to be served in the mansions of the city that was famous over a hundred years before *Midnight in the Garden of Good and Evil* started its long run on *The New York Times* bestseller list. The label is black and gold on a small clear wine bottle. The orange-colored liquid flecked with black pepper beckons you to try it. Non-Southerners will find the flavor as unusual as the book the town made famous. Southerners will recognize the savory, subtle spiciness and will be pleased by the herbal finish. Plantation Foods President Pam Sloan credits her grandfather for developing the original recipe in the early 1900s. Before he died, he gave Aunt Ella the recipe. Aunt Ella enhanced it with her own signature, hence its name, Ella's Ultimate. It is a superb example of sauce in the Savannah tradition.

EL PASO CHILE COMPANY OINK OINTMENT
EL PASO, TEXAS

The Old El Paso Chile Company earns high marks for creative packaging and excellence with their outstanding line of barbecue sauces. Old El Paso's trio—Oink Ointment, Dark Secret Molé and Jamaican Me Crazy—covers the spectrum from savory to sweet to fiery. The medley is a survival kit for people who like variety and quality. Oink Ointment is a savory, tangy mustard-based sauce that, although made in Texas, stands up proudly with its Southern cousins. Dr. Pepper syrup gives it a unique accent. As the name suggests, it's an excellent prescription for pork barbecue.

FAMOUS DAVE'S GEORGIA MUSTARD BBQ SAUCE

EDEN PRAIRIE, MINNESOTA

You may wonder how they could produce such a delicious mustard-based sauce in Minnesota. Famous Dave's Georgia Mustard is a result of Famous Dave's BBQ Shack founder Dave Anderson's extensive travel and barbecue research over the past twenty years. Famous Dave's Georgia Mustard BBQ Sauce is good enough to star at pig-pickin' parties south, north, east, or west. The tangy, sweet flavor with a peppery finish is also great on ribs and chicken. Famous Dave's makes a variety of other sauces. Dave's Rich and Sassy BBQ Sauce is a smooth, sweet, tomato-based blend of special spices and herbs. Dave's Texas Pit BBQ Sauce is sweet and peppery with a touch of fire. His Hot Stuff BBQ Sauce delivers mellow heat in a sweet and smoky tomato base.

FLORIBBEAN TROPICAL BARBECUE SAUCE

MIAMI, FLORIDA

Scotch Bonnet peppers in the ingredients list may lead you to expect Floribbean to be a fiery sauce. It isn't. Scotch Bonnets lend a gentle, tingly finish to Floribbean. Rather than burning, the peppers enhance the tangy, sweet tropical fruit base of the sauce. Guava and papaya purée give Floribbean a refreshing, out-of-the-mainstream flavor. This tropical sauce from an "Old Carribbean Recipe" is versatile as a marinade (thinned with lime juice), finishing sauce, or dipping sauce with pork, poultry, and seafood.

GATES BAR-B-Q SAUCE
KANSAS CITY, MISSOURI

How could such an uncomplicated sauce have such a huge following? To many people, Gates is the definitive sauce of Kansas City. The signature base flavor is a simple combination of tomato purée with accents of powdered cumin, cayenne pepper, and celery seed. At first bite, you may wonder what all the fuss is about. Later you'll wonder how you've done without it. Although Gates is served on all varieties of meat, it's best on beef. You can get it in mild, hot, and extra hot. The Polynesian style, laced with pineapple juice, is excellent on pork ribs, pork sandwiches, and turkey. Pick your favorite Gates sauce and go "struttin' with some barbecue."

BIG BOB GIBSON BAR-B-Q
ORIGINAL WHITE SAUCE
DECATUR, ALABAMA

Big Bob Gibson Bar-B-Q Original White Sauce has been an Alabama tradition since 1925. Bob Gibson's grandson, Don McLemore, continues Big Bob's legacy into the twenty-first century. Alabamans have complemented their barbecue pork and chicken with white sauce for years. Finally the secret is getting out to a larger audience. The sauce is thin textured. From the bottle it tastes like vinegar and mayonnaise accented with black pepper, poppy seeds, and secret spices. It's magical as a marinade and dipping sauce with chicken or pork.

More than seventy years after Bob Gibson developed the white sauce, his heirs have introduced a new tomato-based Big Bob Gibson Sweet Mash Blend Bar-B-Q Sauce. The balance of sweet and sour, accented with traditional and secret flavors, would make Bob Gibson proud. For people who like a sweeter sauce, the family has introduced the excellent new Big Bob Gibson Red Sauce, voted Best on the Planet in 1998.

GOLDEN WHISK
A.J.'S FRISCO B-B-Q
SUPERB SAUCE

SAN FRANCISCO, CALIFORNIA

Shake it well and patiently pour this fabulous thick savory condiment with a panAsian accent, loads of garlic, a hint of nutty flavor, and a slight tangy bite of pepper fire. With this and other bold sauces, Elinor Hill-Courtney has earned a royal culinary title, "Queen of the Kitchen." Her standard is a golden whisk. A. J.'s Frisco B-B-Q Superb Sauce takes a refreshing departure from heavy tomato-based sauces. It is loaded with garlic, touched by "Macho Mesquite," and laced with Elinor's secret "Power Spices." This sauce is best with chicken, pork, fish, and seafood.

AMAZING GRACE'S
BAR-B-Q SAUCE

KANSAS CITY, MISSOURI

Grace Harris's famous barbecue has made her a living Kansas City legend. Blues and jazz musicians from all over the globe have jammed at Grace's place all night long after finishing their paid gigs. The jammin' was fueled with Grace's ribs and sauce. Today she slathers her ribs with her "Best in the U.S.A." barbecue sauce at Kansas City's hot spot for an eclectic variety of top-notch live music, the Grand Emporium. Amazing Grace's tomato-based Bar-B-Q Sauce lends a spicy, tangy complement with a pepper accent to ribs, chicken, and beef.

GUIDO'S SERIOUS
B.B.Q. SAUCE

PASADENA, CALIFORNIA

Guido Meindl knows sauce. From his childhood in Munich, Germany, to over forty years of residence in Pasadena, California, Guido has been dedicated to cooking good food. He got serious about making and selling barbecue sauce in 1994, with the creation of Guido's International Foods. Guido's award-winning barbecue sauce has a thick, rich, red tomato base with a slightly chunky texture. It delivers a spicy, peppery, slightly tangy complement to barbecued meats. A dash of tequila and some secret spices give Guido's a distinctive signature flavor. In addition to barbecue, Guido's is great with baked beans, meat loaf, and a variety of other dishes. It is, as Guido says, "A sauce for all seasons, a sauce for all reasons."

JOHNNY HARRIS FAMOUS BAR-B-CUE SAUCE
SAVANNAH, GEORGIA

A lot of sauce has gone over Savannahians' palates since the Johnny Harris Restaurant was established in 1924. Other, less remarkable, events happened the same year. Calvin Coolidge was reelected to a second term; Macy's had its first Thanksgiving Day Parade; Sak's Fifth Avenue opened; "Little Orphan Annie," Kleenex, and Wheaties were born. A popular song was "Hard Hearted Hannah, The Vamp of Savannah."

You can taste the the richness of Southern tradition in Johnny Harris Famous Bar-B-Cue Sauce. The slightly thick texture sticks well to meat. The tangy, spicy flavor comes from an artful blend of tomato ketchup, prepared mustard, Worcestershire sauce, black pepper, secret spices, and a touch of hickory smoke. Johnny Harris Famous Bar-B-Cue Sauce has been one of my favorites since 1984, when Philip L. Donaldson, company executive, sent me a bottle for the First Annual Diddy-Wa-Diddy National Barbecue Sauce Contest.

D. L. JARDINE'S CHIK'N LIK'N BAR-B-Q SAUCE
BUDA, TEXAS

This Texas sauce is as at home at a Southern pig pickin' as at a Texas chicken lickin'. D. L. Jardine's Chik'n Lik'n Bar-B-Q Sauce's mustard and vinegar in a tomato base gives it tang, with a hint of sweetness. The peppery Southern-style flavor is an excellent complement to barbecued pork and chicken. A splash of D. L. Jardine's Texas Champagne Pepper Sauce adds a perfect finish. Another excellent sauce for chicken and pig is D. L. Jardine's Margarita Bar-B-Q Sauce. This complex, chunky combination of quality herbs, spices, onions, vinegar, peppers, and lime juice with tequila finish can also liven up tender, slow-smoked Texas brisket.

JO B'S GRILLE CARIBE
WARREN, VERMONT

Jo B's creates some of the more eclectic sauces on the market, from Fire Bean Mud Paste, Chilliuna Dipping Sauce, and Black Magic Asian Grill Sauce to Diablo Asado (a chipotle-flavored barbecue sauce), Grille Caribe, and several other varieties. The Grill Caribe sauce has an unexpected sweetness from the addition of papaya; cilantro provides a bit of pungency; and fresh habañero peppers add just enough zip for this to be almost considered a hot sauce. It will keep surprising you with hints of other flavors from the twenty-six different ingredients found in it, such as dark rum, molasses, cider vinegar, and soy sauce. Consider this sauce for multiple duties—as a baste or a dipping sauce, or splash it on as a condiment. Although Jo B's is made in Vermont, it has a taste that is direct from the Caribbean.

KRAFT ORIGINAL BARBECUE SAUCE
GLENVIEW, ILLINOIS

Kraft Original has earned a niche in history as the classic American barbecue sauce. It is the giant of the industry. If you've detoured from Kraft in search of new flavors and variety, it's time to revisit. Kraft's smooth, tangy, peppered tomato base with an herbal finish is versatile enough to complement your entire spectrum of grilled and barbecued meats. This classic sauce is a base for hundreds of secret sauces concocted by backyard pitmasters and competition barbecue cooking teams. Kraft Thick and Spicy Original is thicker and slightly sweeter. Both carry a subtle hint of hickory smoke. For more smoke flavor, Kraft offers Hickory Smoke Barbecue Sauce.

Kraft Thick and Spicy Cajun takes a distinct departure from original. It is slightly sweeter, textured, and flavored with bell peppers and onion, Cajun herbs, spices, and hot peppers. It is mild, but it bites.

Kraft's outstanding sweeter sauces include smoky Kansas City Style with a peppery finish, Steakhouse Style, Thick and Spicy Brown Sugar, Honey, Spicy Honey, and Honey Mustard.

KINGS DELIGHT BARBEQUE SAUCE
KINSTON, NORTH CAROLINA

Although the "stuff" the late Wilbur King Sr. put in this sauce is expensive, Wilbur King Jr. refuses to compromise the recipe. He makes it just like Daddy did. Wilbur admits to trying to make it cheaper, but "with no success. No go. Can't do it."

Kings Delight is the hallmark of Eastern North Carolina vinegar-based barbecue sauces. These sauces reflect a colonial tradition at least as old as Washington and Jefferson. They are more authentically American than today's tomato-based favorites. If you've never tried a vinegar-based sauce, Kings is the best place to begin. Although the signature flavor is vinegar, it delivers a robust, spicy combination that will gently bite you and make your lips tingle with pleasure.

THE ORIGINAL
KING STREET BLUES
MAHOGANY BARBECUE SAUCE

VIRGINIA BEACH, VIRGINIA

At the King Street Blues Restaurant in Alexandria, Virginia, the house barbecue sauce is a tangy, spicy Mahogany. It is just the right thickness to stick to your ribs or your pork sandwich. After the initial spicy hit on your palate, the sauce has an herbal finish. It also contains a small amount of bourbon as a flavor enhancer. The same chile-tomato sauce base comes in a sweeter version called Watermelon. You can taste sweet, tiny, pieces of pickled watermelon rind. The label on both sauces carries a warning that "a delicious addiction for which there is no known cure" could result from consumption of the sauce. Go ahead and get addicted.

LINDSAY FARMS
SPECIALTIES VIDALIA ONION
BARBECUE SAUCE

ATLANTA, GEORGIA

Although a duck adorns the label, this sauce is outstanding with slow-smoked Georgia pig. The tomato base is made tangy with vinegar and lemon juice. Pieces of sweet Vidalia onion lend a special texture and flavor that is complemented by pepper and secret spices. Put this sauce on pork and chicken as a finishing and dipping sauce.

MASON'S OLD MILL
BARBECUE CAROLINA
MUSTARD SAUCE

ELKHORN, NEBRASKA

Sauces developed by Mason Steinberg benefit from his persistent, meticulous attention to detail. This includes historical research and networking with other professional and competition pitmasters. Carolina Mustard is my favorite of Mason's Old

Mill line of barbecue products. It isn't fancy. It isn't meant to be. Its job is to complement the flavor of barbecued meat, especially pork and chicken. It does this by balancing the sweetness of pit-smoked pulled pork with the tangy flavor of mustard, vinegar, savory spices, a touch of sugar, and garlic. With barbecued beef I prefer Mason's Old Mill tomato-based sauces. The sweetness in the mild and the hot versions brings out the flavor in barbecued beef.

MATT'S SHARK SHACK ARM LICKIN' BBQ SAUCE

RALEIGH, NORTH CAROLINA

Somebody remarked, "This sauce is good enough to lick off your arm." After that, Matt's Shark Shack BBQ Sauce was known as Arm Lickin' BBQ Sauce. The sauce was so popular at the state fair and everywhere else they introduced it, that it grew from a family favorite to a commercial success. Shark Shack's smooth tomato base is laced with bits of onion, pepper, and spices. The tangy sweetness of Matt's Shark Shack Arm Lickin' BBQ Sauce lends a perfect complement to pork and chicken. A hint of mustard and a little bit of pepper heat gives it a great finish. If you're hairy, try not to spill Matt's on your arms. You could get a hairball.

McILHENNY FARMS SOUTH LOUISIANA STYLE BAR-B-QUE SAUCE

AVERY ISLAND, LOUISIANA

This beautiful sauce from the makers of Tabasco brand hot sauce is not for dipping. It is a basting and finishing sauce. McIlhenny Farms South Louisiana Style Bar-B-Que Sauce is thick, chunky, slightly tangy, with a complex, distinctive flavor accented with bite from the famous Tabasco red peppers. Use it according to the directions on the label, and you'll be rewarded with some flavorful, break-from-the-rut barbecue.

MAURICE'S GOURMET BLEND BBQ SAUCE
WEST COLUMBIA, SOUTH CAROLINA

You'll never forget your first taste of mustard-based barbecue sauce. For most people, the first taste is Maurice's Gourmet Blend Carolina Gold BBQ Sauce. It is a world apart from tomato-based sauces. Maurice's is pig sauce. It isn't meant for barbecued beef brisket. It is meant for pig: pig sandwiches, pig meat loaf, pig ribs. They sell it from a home base called Piggie Park. If you've never tried pig with Maurice's, you've missed a whole dimension of pig cuisine. How does it taste? It will zing you with the tang of apple cider vinegar, then follow with smooth, mellow sweetness reminiscent of ballpark mustard on a hot dog with pickle relish. Try it on hot dogs. Try it in stew. Try it on your grits. And of course, try it on your pig. It's a regular at my house.

JACK MIXON'S OLD SOUTH BAR-B-QUE SAUCE
VIENNA, GEORGIA

A few years ago at the Memphis in May festival, the Jack Mixon's Old South Bar-B-Que team cooked one of the finest whole hogs I've ever eaten. Besides knowing how to cook a hog, this team from Vienna, Georgia, knew exactly how much spicy vinegar-based sauce to serve with the meat. Sweet pork meat with Jack Mixon's Old South Bar-B-Que Sauce is a perfect combination. The Mixon family adapted their recipe from an old Carolina recipe, which was used in Carolina as a mopping sauce on hogs that were slow-cooked the old-fashioned way—buried underground with hot coals. The hot version of the original recipe is spicier but won't hurt you. A recent variation from the original recipe is the addition of fruits and natural sweeteners in a sauce called Tangy Sweet. All three Jack Mixon sauces are exceptional on pork and chicken.

MONTEZUMA SMOKEY & SPICY BARBECUE SAUCE

COLUMBUS, OHIO

Chuck Evans, founder of Sauces & Salsas, Ltd., has a gift for making sauce. One of his award-winning favorites is Montezuma Smokey & Spicy Barbecue Sauce. The tangy, peppery, tomato-based sauce laced with vinegar is loaded with flavor. Although smoked jalapeño (chipotle) is a signature accent, the sauce is mild enough for people who don't like fire. Use Montezuma on all of your favorite barbecue foods for an extraordinary twist on old favorites. Sauces & Salsas, Ltd., makes a variety of other barbecue sauces, marinades, salsas, and hot sauces, from mild to fiery.

MOONLITE INN BAR-B-Q SAUCE

OWENSBORO, KENTUCKY

They call this sauce "A Kentucky Tradition." Moonlite could also be called a Kentucky legend, a Kentucky masterpiece—and, for many, a Kentucky necessity. As a necessity, it's required far beyond the Kentucky border by legions of fans who have tried it and can't do without it. Although Owensboro is known as the lamb barbecue capital of the world, Moonlite is a fabulous complement to more than lamb. The smooth, tangy, mellow spicing of Moonlite, accented with a touch of vodka, does an outstanding job on pork shoulder, pork ribs, beef brisket, chicken, hamburgers, sausage, turkey, duck, and wild game. Moonlite has been a necessity at my house for many years.

MR. SPICE HONEY BBQ BARBEQUE SAUCE

NEWPORT, RHODE ISLAND

David Lang stepped ahead of the sauce pack with a brilliant innovation: no salt! Yet that doesn't mean no flavor. Mr. Spice Honey BBQ Barbeque Sauce satisfies your flavor buds with an award-winning tomato-based blend of chile peppers, secret spices, and a smooth apple cider vinegar tang. A hint of sweet clover honey adds a pleasant balance. David, known as "Mr. Spice," also makes a variety of other sauces—steak sauce, curry sauce, peanut sauce, stir-fry sauce, and hot sauces.

NEELY'S BAR-B-Q SAUCE
MEMPHIS, TENNESSEE

Three generations of Neelys have been cranking out world-class barbecue that is matched only by their world-class sauce. This old family recipe is a thick, dark sauce that has been slow simmered to bring out the many different flavoring components. Corn syrup and brown sugar makes the sauce lean a bit to the sweet side, but cider vinegar makes Neely's stay on the mid-South side of tanginess. Neely's thick, smooth tomato base carries a heavy hit of smoke, folded into a complex blend of peppers and spices. This versatile sauce makes for a great baste on any barbecued or grilled meat, poultry or seafood. Brothers Tony, Patrick, Mark, and Gaelin Neely call their family restaurant "Memphis' best kept secret." The more their sauce gets slathered on barbecue pork, however, the less the secret will be kept. Neely's makes a great "sopping" sauce. You won't want to miss a drop of this Memphis classic!

OAK HILL FARMS VIDALIA ONION BARBECUE SAUCE
ATLANTA, GEORGIA

Oak Hill Farms brings classy packaging and sophisticated flavors to the sauce market. Oak Hill Farms Vidalia Onion Barbecue Sauce is elegantly labeled in black and gold. The smooth, sweet, and tangy tomato-based barbecue sauce lends a sophisticated complement to any barbecue meat, with a smoky pepper finish. Some sweetness and flavor come from Georgia's famous Vidalia onions. If you want fire in your sauce, add Oak Hill Farms Scorned Woman Hot Sauce.

OMAHA STEAKS HICKORY
OMAHA, NEBRASKA

This sauce, made by the same company that brings you legendary steaks, shows they know how to make great sauce as well. This savory blend has a little bit of sweet to it that is just right for a baste, but you'll want to set some aside for dipping later. Although steak isn't the first meat that comes to mind for barbecue sauce, I used this sauce in the last two minutes of cooking as a baste and then let the steaks sit a few minutes before cutting to absorb the juices and to let the flavors mingle. Wonderful!

GENUINE ROADKILL BAR-B-Q SAUCE
SHAWNEE MISSION, KANSAS

Tasting this sauce and reading its label is not likely to inspire you to harvest the next dead rabbit you see at the side of the road. If you are so inclined, there are directions on the label for preparing and cooking rabbit, skunk, opossum, road hen, deer, moose, bear, pigeon, squirrel, or armadillo. The only concession to food safety is this warning: "If it tastes too strong its been dead too long."

My advice is to ignore roadkill but use the sauce. Used sparingly as a finishing sauce on chicken or pork, the thick tomatoey taste laced with vinegar, spices, and a hint of liquid smoke will bring home the flavor.

ROWENA'S COOKING & BARBECUE SAUCE
NORFOLK, VIRGINIA

The word wholesome came to mind with my first bite of Rowena's on a pork sandwich. Rowena's is gentle, ketchupy, tangy, with tiny chunks of vegetables and herbs that taste like they came fresh from a well-tended garden. It is great on any barbecued meat and on a variety of other foods.

RUMBOGGIES BAR-B-QUE SAUCE
JACKSONVILLE, FLORIDA

The late J. C. Bearden was a truck driver with a reputation for making outstanding home brew. He was nicknamed "Rumboogies." He spelled it, "Rumboggies." When J. C.'s son Roger and Roger's wife, Cecilia, perfected this Southern-style sauce for their Jacksonville, Florida, restaurant, they named the restaurant and the sauce, Rumboggies. The sauce is straightforward: It does what it's meant to do. Rumboggies Mild is a tangy mustard sauce that is packed with flavor. It is smooth-textured, flecked with red spices in a pumpkin-colored mustard mixed with vinegar, ketchup, and secret spices. I liked Rumboggies at first bite and ever after. Rumboggies Hot has the same wonderful flavor as the mild, with a gentle afterburn. Sweet Hickory is the original flavor made almost as sweet as candy. Rumboggies is an excellent sauce and has international awards to prove it. It's best with barbecued pork and chicken.

SAGUARO COOL COYOTE SMOKIN' BBQ & MARINADE SAUCE
TUCSON, ARIZONA

Although they call the other sauces in the Cool Coyote line either glazes or grill and marinade sauces, I've found them to be equally good as dipping sauces for barbecue. The tomato-based Cool Coyote Smokin' BBQ Sauce, darkened and flavored with rich molasses, smoked jalapeños, fresh onions, cider vinegar, a touch of fresh orange, and secret spices, is a versatile, all-around barbecue sauce for people who prefer tangy to sweet.

Ray and Georgia Pisciotta, co-owners, bought Saguaro when it was a potato and tortilla chip company. Georgia formulated dips and sauces to expand the product line and introduce some refreshing new flavors for your backyard barbecue. Try Saguaros Arizona Sunset Grill & Marinade Sauce for a zesty lemon and pepper accent on grilled chicken, seafood, or fresh fish; Mango-Jalapeño Grilling & Broiling Glaze for an excellent sweet/hot complement to grilled chicken or barbecued pork; Prickly Pear Grill & Marinade Sauce for a peppery, spicy smoke flavor; Pineapple Jalapeño Grilling & Broiling Glaze for a sweet and spicy pineapple accent; and Grand Canyon Gourmet Hickory Grill & Marinade Sauce for a savory, slightly sweet, bold, hickory flavor.

SAUER'S BARBECUE SAUCE
RICHMOND, VIRGINIA

If there's a hog heaven for pitmasters, Sauer's Barbecue Sauce is surely on the table. This barbecue sauce "from an old Southern recipe" is versatile enough to mop, finish, and dip. The tangy vinegar base is mellowed with tomato, sugar, salt, mustard, and secret spices that give it a signature finish. I like Sauer's best on pork barbecue of any kind. It is also recommended for all meats and seafood. For more bite, try Sauer's Hot.

SHEALY'S BAR-B-QUE SAUCE
LEESVILLE, SOUTH CAROLINA

I am forever grateful to my barbecue cousin, Fred Davis, for telling me about Shealy's Bar-B-Que Sauce. It was a favorite at first bite. Shealy's is a mustard sauce in the tradition of the South Carolina midlands. It was developed by Victor and Sara Shealy in the 1950s, when they started barbecuing in their backyard. They established Shealy's Bar-B-Que Restaurant in 1969 on, as Todd Shealy says, "a nickel and a prayer." Victor quit his job as a night watchman and Sara quit her pharmacy job to run the restaurant. Their hard work, "crowd-pleasing" sauce, and quality food paid off. Shealy's grew to a restaurant that seats over 350 people and has over 75 employees. If you have trouble with the idea of yellow barbecue sauce, let yourself stretch. The smooth, tangy, complex, spicy flavor of Shealy's could easily make it one of your favorites. Use it as a dipping sauce with pork barbecue and chicken. Okay, use it on hot dogs too. You'll taste why Shealy's is an award winner.

SNAKE PIT
BARBEQUE SAUCE
ILLINOIS

This sauce appeared in my mailbox one day, without an accompanying letter and without a fancy package or label, but the sauce is quite tasty. It's dark and slightly sweet, with a pleasant afterburn from chile peppers. The sauce is apparently available in Illinois, where I can't tell you, but if you get the chance to "get snake bit with snake pit" (as the label states), buy some. This sauce is a great example of high-quality sauce made in small quantities, a classic collector's sauce.

THE STINKING ROSE
GARLIC BARBEQUE SAUCE
SAN FRANCISCO, CALIFORNIA

A sign in the doorway of the Stinking Rose reads, "for people who like a little food with their garlic." The Stinking Rose is a wildly popular restaurant located in the North Beach area of San Francisco, and their barbecue sauce is just the ticket for those garlic fans out there that can't stand the notion of any food not being kissed by their beloved "stinking rose." The sauce is a dark, smooth blend of garlic, in the powdered and fresh form. Well, they do put a few other items in there. Ketchup, cider vinegar, and Worcestershire sauce all make major contributions. The sauce is quite thick and performed very nicely brushed on beef and pork ribs, although chicken would certainly fare just as well. The garlic flavor is apparent but not overbearing, so you garlic fiends may want to add more finely chopped or puréed garlic.

STUBB'S LEGENDARY
BAR-B-QUE SAUCE
AUSTIN, TEXAS

"Ladies and Gentlemen, I am a cook!" is what the late Mr. C. B. Stubblefield proudly declares on each bottle of his famous sauce. When you've lived with Stubb's sauce for a while, you'll agree that this man was indeed a cook. Stubb's is a great all-purpose barbecue sauce for beef, pork, chicken, hot links, sausage, and much more. It excels with barbecued beef brisket. Stubb's is an authentic tomato-based, pepper-laced Texas barbecue sauce. It isn't sweet. If you like sweet, Stubb's will take a while to get used to.

THOMAS SAUCE
GREENSBORO, NORTH CAROLINA

Its makers say, "Thomas Sauce was born in a bowl in rural North Carolina back in the early thirties about midway between the mountains and the sea." Tomato adds balance and texture to this thin, popular barbecue sauce with a Worcestershire sauce signature. Although Thomas promises not to be "heavy-handed," the tangy burst of pepper at first bite doesn't sneak up on you. Use Thomas Sauce sauce on your barbecued pork sandwiches and ribs, and on grilled steaks and burgers. Use it on other foods. Be creative. They call it a "North Carolina sauce for food and imagination."

THUNDER BAY BRAZILIAN
MUSTARD GLAZE
PORTSMOUTH, VIRGINIA

Most stores stock Thunder Bay on the barbecue sauce shelves, although Chefs Chris and Loeticia St. James don't label their "glaze" as such. I like to use Thunder Bay Brazilian Mustard Glaze as a finishing and dipping sauce with pork and chicken. Mustard seed, poppy seed, citrus peel, and coarsely ground spices lend texture, flavor, and eye appeal. Apple cider vinegar gives Thunder Bay a tangy accent. The sauce is sweetened with sugar and tamarinds, and finishes with a distant thunder of fieriness.

UNCLE DAVE'S KICKIN' GRILL SAUCE

SOUTH LONDONDERRY, VERMONT

As much a barbecue sauce as a "grill sauce," Uncle Dave's kick comes from fresh flavors, not fiery peppers. Apple-smoked onion pieces with apple cider vinegar, tamari, molasses, vegetarian Worcestershire sauce, and secret spices in a tomato paste base make Uncle Dave's an outstanding dipping sauce. It's especially good with pork, beef, and chicken.

VAN'S PIG STAND BARBEQUE SAUCE

SHAWNEE, OKLAHOMA

Van's stands on the line between sweet and tangy. Ketchup and brown sugar pull it in the sweet direction, but apple cider vinegar pushes it to the tangy side. All the better, since it appeals to both sweet and tangy eaters. Lots of folks like it, and have since Leroy Vandegrift invented it at the age of twenty-three in the summer of 1919. At the time, Leroy had set up a barbecue tent in an oil field near Burkburnett, Texas. By 1928, Leroy opened the first Van's in Oklahoma. He moved the business from Wewoka to Seminole and finally to Shawnee. In Shawnee he met and married Thelma Glenn. Stability, popularity, and growth followed. Since 1978, Van's has prospered under the management of Leroy and Thelma's son, Jerry. Jerry has been involved in the family pig stand business since 1959. Van's tangy, sweet smooth and spicy combo with a pepper and cinnamon finish is unequaled on ribs, brisket, steak, and chicken. You can get Van's shipped nationwide to your house, RV, apartment, or tent in original mild or bite-your-tongue hot.

CHARLIE VERGOS RENDEZVOUS FAMOUS BARBECUE SAUCE

MEMPHIS, TENNESSEE

Everyone who goes to Memphis should go down the alley across the street from the main entrance of the Peabody Hotel, and downstairs to the Rendezvous. When you enter, you are greeted with the aroma of charcoal smoke and walls covered with memorabilia. The place pulsates with the hustle and bustle of bow-tied waiters and the animated chatter of hundreds of happy diners. The ambiance is exciting, but what you go to Charlie's place for is the flavor of Charlie Vergos's own Memphis-style grilled baby backs slathered in Famous Barbecue Sauce or sprinkled with Famous Seasoning.

When you open a bottle of this famous sauce, the aroma of spice, vinegar, and tomato will immediately urge you to eat barbecue. The smooth, burnt-orange liquid is filled with tiny flecks of peppers and other spices. The zesty sweet blend of vinegar, tomato, and peppers includes a slight accent of hot pepper. This sauce is especially good on barbecued pork ribs and pork shoulder, but it's also delicious with beef, chicken, and lamb. I call it "Memphis in a bottle." Although I live in Kansas City, Rendezvous Famous Sauce and Seasoning is a regular on my table.

WICKER'S THICKER BARBECUE SAUCE

HORNERSVILLE, MISSOURI

Several generations of Missourians have regarded Wicker's as synonymous with barbecue. The classic Wicker's Marinade and Baste is a staple throughout Missouri and the mid-South. Use Wicker's Thicker barbecue Sauce after meat has been marinated and basted with original Wicker's. The combination is unbeatable. Tomato paste, lots of vinegar, a slight touch of brown sugar sweetness, and a blend of spices reminiscent of the Marinade spices make Wicker's Thicker great with most any meat.

FIERY SAUCES

ACID RAIN BARBECUE SAUCE

SHAWNEE MISSION, KANSAS

Described as the "Paint Remover of Barbecue Sauce," Acid Rain is not to be dismissed as a novelty sauce. It is a legitimate flavor enhancer for your barbecue meats. Acid Rain is on the sweet side of Kansas City style, in a tomato base, with enough fire from habañero and cayenne peppers to live up to its name. Don't worry about the metal cap corroding. You'll run out of sauce before corrosion can set in.

ALLEGRO CREOLE MARINADE AND SEASONING

PARIS, TENNESSEE

This is my favorite of the outstanding line of Allegro products. Although Allegro is marketed as a marinade, I prefer its upbeat flavor straight from the bottle as a barbecue sauce. The thin soy sauce base is flavored with the stimulating Creole herbs, spices, and peppers popular in Southern Louisiana. The chile pepper fire is gentle, not excessive, and the soy sauce as a base gives Allegro an international appeal. Dave Wilcox, founder and president of Allegro Fine Foods, generously invests part of his profits back into the local community through college and university scholarships and a program for ex-convicts.

ANNIE CHUN'S ALL NATURAL HOT & SPICY TERIYAKI BARBEQUE SAUCE

SAUSALITO, CALIFORNIA

Annie Chun's delivers the rich flavor of a soy sauce base, with the health benefit of less sodium. Lots of toasted sesame seeds, garlic, a hint of celery, and the slow burn of peppers that eventually zaps you make Annie Chun's an outstanding soy-based barbecue sauce. It works great as a marinade, baste, finishing sauce, and dipping sauce. Annie Chun's also makes a variety of sauces for other uses, such as stir-fry, noodles, and salad dressings. The sauces were adapted from old family recipes that reflect Annie's experience of living half of her life in Korea and half in Northern California. The sauce makes outstanding Korean-style beef, ribs, and chicken.

AUNT BEA'S HOT & TANGY BARBECUE SAUCE

MOUNT AIRY, NORTH CAROLINA

Aunt Bea's has the authentic flavor of a tangy, peppery North Carolina vinegar sauce. Thickened with tomato concentrate and fired with cayenne pepper, it is the only barbecue sauce I've discovered that contains turnips. When Fred Jones and Ted Beaver established Aunt Bea's Barbecue Restaurant in Mt. Airy in 1984, they developed Aunt Bea's Hot & Tangy Barbecue Sauce as a shaker sauce for customers to use at the table. As a marinade, mopping sauce, dipping or shaker sauce, Aunt Bea's is a great complement to slow-smoked chopped or pulled pork shoulder. It also goes well on chicken, beef, game meats, pork ribs, and beans.

BAR-B-Q HEAVEN
ALL PURPOSE SAUCE
INDIANAPOLIS, INDIANA

Ronald F. Jones is a veteran barbecue pitmaster in a city that is better known for race car pits than for barbecue pits. Bar-B-Q Heaven has been "famous since 1952." Part of their secret has to be the sauce. Mr. Jones makes the original family recipe sauce in three varieties—mild, sweet, and hot. Each is a variation on the original recipe in a tomato base. The mild is slightly sweet and spicy, with a peppery bite at the finish. The sweet is less spicy than the mild. The hot hits you up front with spices and follows with lip-tingling fire. This sauce goes well with all barbecued meats and other foods, and the tomato base has a good texture for finishing and dipping.

BIG RICK'S BIG TASTE
BAR-B-Q SAUCE
WICHITA, KANSAS

The trademark slogan for Big Rick's Big Taste Bar-B-Q Sauce is "Big guys always have the best eats." Big or not, Rick Doty makes great sauce. He developed the sauce out of necessity, after what he says was a futile search for a good hot barbecue sauce in Wichita, Kansas. Big Rick's smooth, glossy original flavor is a mild version of Rick's antidote to the hot barbecue sauce void in the Air Capital of the World. The sweet, brilliantly seasoned condiment, textured with chopped onions, has a gentle fiery finish fueled by chile peppers. Fiery eaters who like sweetness smacked with habañeros should add Big Rick's hot version to their weekly shopping list.

BOZO'S HOT PIT BAR-B-QUE SAUCE

MASON, TENNESSEE

The late Thomas Jefferson "Bozo" Williams started Bozo's Hot Pit Bar-B-Que Restaurant in 1923. Several fires and new buildings later, the restaurant still serves some of the best pig sandwiches on the planet. Jeff Thompson, Mr. Williams's great grandson, now runs Bozo's, and he is dedicated to continuing the Bozo legacy. Jeff knows the recipe for Bozo's original hot barbecue sauce by heart. The only difference from the 1920s is that today's Bozo Sauce is not served in a whiskey bottle. This sauce is made for pig sandwiches, the only barbecue sold at Bozo's. You can get the pig white, brown, or mixed. Brown is the crusty "bark" from outside the shoulder. White is the inside. Both are excellent, so get mixed. The sauce is vinegar-based, thin, spicy, and fiery. Sprinkle it in moderation until you figure out how much Bozo fire you can handle. Bozo's also offers a respectable sweeter, mild, tomato-based sauce. If you can't go to Mason, Tennessee, near Memphis, send for Bozo's sauce and put it on your own shoulders and ribs. It isn't fancy. It's just good sauce.

BUTCH'S CHAMPIONSHIP B-B-Q SAUCE

MOUNT LAUREL, NEW JERSEY

"Butch" Lupinetti dukes it out each year on the rib-burning circuit with a few score other hardworking, friendly, masterful barbecue ambassadors. Butch has won awards at all of the major rib cookoffs. His home base is New Jersey. His sauce base is tomato. Beyond tomato, Butch does his magic with sugar, vinegars, sauces, spices, lemon juice, and garlic powder. His sauce sticks to your ribs and enhances the flavor. Butch's regular sauce is mild, sweet and tangy with a peppery finish. The Pyrogenic and Super Pyro also carry Butch's signature sweet, tangy, peppery finish, but with a lot of fire. Each is certified at 500,000 and 1,000,000 Scovilles, respectively. They will wake up your ribs and slap your tongue. Be careful.

CRAIG'S CHIPOTLE SAUCE
CRANFORD, NEW JERSEY

Craig's compares to ordinary barbecue sauces as wild straw-berries compare to truck farm berries. A small bottle of Craig's packs more flavor than a case of ordinary others. An artful blend of chipotle peppers, habañero, vinegar, brown sugar, peaches, secret herbs, and spices, Craig's is an instant palate pleaser, even to people who think they won't like a hot barbecue sauce. Go easy with the first bite, or you'll imitate the screaming chilehead on the Craig's label. Craig's gives a spicy, herbal complement to barbe-cued meats and vegetables. The heat doesn't burn out your taste buds. It's fire, but it's friendly fire. Craig and Cindy Neivert modestly call it, "New Jersey's Finest." You don't need Craig's first place honors at the 1997 Fiery Foods Show to confirm that this sauce is one of Mother Earth's finest.

DANCING PIGS
HOT BAR-B-QUE SAUCE
MEMPHIS, TENNESSEE

Frank and Hazel Vernon, and their son Eric, are the owners of the Bar-B-Q Shop in Memphis, Tennessee. Their sauce, which they call Dancing Pigs Bar-B-Que Sauce, was developed from recipes that are over fifty years old. The Bar-B-Q Shop, first known as Brady and Lil's Bar-B-Q Restaurant, has been oper-ated by the Vernon family for over a quarter of a century. It is famous in Memphis and beyond. Frank Vernon attributes the fame to the Bar-B-Q Shop's "unique taste of barbecue." He says, further, that the restaurant's "unique taste would not have been as delicious had it not been for our barbecue sauce." You can trust the "Hot" designation on Dancing Pigs Hot Bar-B-Q Sauce. The Vernons lace the savory mustard base with enough fire and spice to put your pigs in the mosh pit. Dancing Pigs Original Bar-B-Q Sauce, however, is more suitable for waltzing. It is sweeter, with a tomato base and the signature spices of the Bar-B-Q Shop, minus pepper fire. Naturally, pork is the meat of choice for Dancing Pigs, but beef and chicken are no wallflowers with it either.

DAVE'S GOURMET BADLANDS BARBEQUE SAUCE

SAN BRUNO, CALIFORNIA

Dijon mustard and jalapeño pepper make up the signature flavor combo of this spicy, tangy, sweet condiment with a bodacious pedigree. Compared to the famous Dave's Insanity Sauce and other creative hot sauces produced by Dave, Badlands Barbeque Sauce is mild. Badlands won't send you in search of a microbrewed fire extinguisher, but it will wake up your mouth with spiciness and a jalapeño burn. Badlands works as a marinade, finishing sauce, or dipping sauce on all barbecued and grilled foods. Dave recommends his sauce for burgers, chicken, shrimp, fish, veggies, and pasta. It's also great with a barbecued pork sandwich and on pork ribs. Take the warning on the label seriously: Badlands "may be addictive."

DINOSAUR WANGO TANGO HABAÑERO HOT BAR-B-QUE SAUCE

SYRACUSE, NEW YORK

Dinosaur Bar-B-Q in Syracuse, New York, is known for its eclectic decor, diverse clientele, live blues, and outstanding barbecue. Dinosaur is also known for its sauce. The house Sensuous Slathering Sauce is reviewed in the "Sweet" section of this book. Wango Tango will grab your attention at first bite. It doesn't wait to sneak up on you. It hits you immediately with cayenne pepper fire, followed by a rush of habañero peppers. Unlike some hot sauces that bomb your taste buds, Wango Tango's pepper fire, in a lightly spiced tomato base with a hint of smoke, enhances the flavor of barbecued meat. Wango Tango tangos with ribs, chicken, pulled or chopped pork, beef, shrimp, and fish.

GOLDWATER'S BISBEE BARBEQUE SAUCE
SCOTTSDALE, ARIZONA

This medium-fiery tomato-based sauce combines traditional flavors of Worcestershire sauce, molasses, and vinegar with a Southwestern accent of smoky chipotle peppers and secret spices. Textured to stick to your meat, Goldwater's Bisbee delivers a wake-up call to hot-off-the grill chicken or fresh from the pit brisket. Since Arizona produces more copper than any other state in the United States, it is fitting that Goldwater's named this sauce for one of the early copper mining boomtowns near the Mexico-Arizona border. Bisbee, in those days, was known for its rowdiness. The bite from smoked and dried jalapeño peppers in this sauce is a fitting reminder of its namesake.

HABAÑERO BBQ SAUCE FROM HELL
GLENDALE, ARIZONA

As you can gather from the name of this sauce, it's hot! The good news, however, is that this "sauce from hell" won't scorch your palate. After you pick up a bit of the burn, a pleasant tangy flavor comes through, followed by a fruity hint of apricot (which probably comes from the habanero peppers). While this sauce is not one for the faint hearted, it won't send your taste buds to the devil. I found the tasty kick perfect for pork and beef ribs. It makes a fine chicken wing sauce too.

HAWAIIAN PASSION SPICY TERIYAKI SAUCE
HAUULA, HAWAII

Henry Holthaus, certified executive chef and instructor at Kapiolani Community College, Hauula, Hawaii, cares more about flavor than fire. This focus has produced award-winning sauces with an international customer base. Henry makes Hawaiian Passion Spicy Teriyaki Sauce for barbecued hog, Hawaiian style. He calls it a "kalbi sauce, intensified with the fiery flavor of chile peppers." Tropical sweetness from lilikoi, pineapple, and sugar blends with soy sauce, ginger, secret spices, and chile peppers to make Hawaiian Passion Spicy Teriyaki Sauce an outstanding complement to barbecued pork. You needn't cook your hog in a buried bed of hot coals to get the benefit of Hawaiian Passion's tropical sweetness and fiery finish. You'll get outstanding results in a regular barbecue pit.

HOG WILD BARBEQUE SAUCE
VIRGINIA BEACH, VIRGINIA

The people who make Hog Wild say it is "distinctly American for the BBQ purist." My definition of a barbecue purist is one who eschews all seasonings except those that result from the action of fire and smoke. That is Native American barbecue purism. Colonial Americans, however, used a seasoned vinegar on their barbecue, so in that sense Hog Wild is for purists. Purist or not, you'll love this sauce. It is thin and vinegary, but more complex than simple vinegar and pepper. The little bit of brown sugar sweetness, the fire from chile peppers, and the pucker of lemon juice make Hog Wild an improvement over purist Colonial sauce. Use Hog Wild for basting, finishing, or sprinkling on your meat, especially hog. When basting, remember the chile peppers—the more you baste, the hotter the meat.

INNER BEAUTY
REAL HOT SAUCE
CAMBRIDGE, MASSACHUSETTS

Life is short. If you need a wake-up call, Inner Beauty will do the job. Inner Beauty puts a fire in your belly, gives your lips a pleasant tingle, and reminds you how important it is to get in touch with the beauty of your inner self before it's too late. It doesn't say "barbecue sauce" or "jerk sauce" on the label, but that's how I met this sauce and that's how I use it, and that's what it is. Inner Beauty's aggressive combination of mustard with tropical flavors—a touch of sweetness, secret spices, and, of course, the signature wallop of scotch bonnet peppers—is excellent as a dipping sauce with barbecued chicken and pork. It's also great with grilled seafood or freshwater fish. Use Inner Beauty in moderation for best results. Many famous entertainers are in love with this sauce. Inner Beauty will remind you, however, that, in the words of the late great singer-songwriter Townes Van Zandt, "Love Hurts!" Applause to Chris Schlesinger, chef/owner of Cambridge's famous East Coast Grill, birthplace of Inner Beauty.

GAUCHO JACK'S ARGENTINIAN GRILLING SAUCE
BURLINGTON, VERMONT

Jack Blumer's uncle was a gaucho in Argentina in 1897. After a long day of herding cattle, the gauchos gathered wood at their campsite, built a huge open pit fire, and barbecued an entire bull or cow. Each gaucho sliced off a large portion of meat, seasoned it with a traditional Argentinian fiery sauce, and devoured it. Jack Blumer makes Gaucho Jack's Argentinian Grilling Sauce from the recipe his uncle brought home and handed down through generations of the Blumer family. Gaucho Jack's excels when applied during the last few minutes of grilling or barbecuing as a finishing sauce. Vinegar, sherry, aged cayenne peppers, chile peppers, ground mustard seed, cinnamon, and garlic, in secret proportions, give Gaucho Jack's an original flavor. It is hot, but not overpowering. Jack Blumer recommends it for steaks, pork, lamb, burgers, chops, and tofu. Gaucho Jack's milder Argentinian Marinade also contains aged cayenne peppers. The spicy flavor is similar to the grilling sauce, with hints of lemon and ginger. It works as a marinade or a finishing sauce, especially on pork, chicken, seafood, and fish.

JAKARTA BALI
BARBEQUE SAUCE

AUSTIN, TEXAS

This fabulous sauce is made in Texas for an Indonesian restaurant in San Francisco. Don't worry about why. Just get the sauce. The fresh blend of sweetened tomato sauce, soy sauce, chile peppers, onion, garlic, and powdered coriander delivers a complex sweet, nutty complement to barbecued chicken, pork, lamb, or beef. Jakarta is also good with grilled foods such as shrimp or fish. Ground dried chile peppers fuel a miniburst of gentle fire.

JAMAICAN ME CRAZY
BARBEQUE SAUCE

EL PASO, TEXAS

Jamaican Me Crazy, a product of the El Paso Chile Company, is good enough to convert people who think they won't like jerk seasoning. Tomatoes, molasses, lime juice, chile peppers, allspice, onion, and other seasonings deliver a sweet, tangy, fiery complement to any grilled or barbecued meat.

D. L. JARDINE'S KILLER
BARBECUE SAUCE

BUDA, TEXAS

D. L. Jardine's has a special talent for matching creative packaging with quality products. The labels look like Texas and talk like Texas. The sauces taste like Texas. Killer is on the macho side of the image. The name is a dare to any chilehead in search of fire. The Special Edition Hot Texas Bar-B-Q Sauce, however, won't bring sweat to the brow of hardcore fireaters. It burns, but not so much that it hurts you or overpowers the flavor of your barbecue. The pepper fire in this slightly sweet tomato-based sauce is rounded out with Worcestershire, vinegar, secret spices, and hickory smoke. Fiery eaters will also like D. L. Jardine's 5-Star Barbecue Sauce. It is sweeter, fired with jalapeño peppers, and has a more complex flavor than Killer. Both sauces are fabulous with slow-smoked Texas-thick slices of tender beef brisket.

JAZZY HOT 'N' SPICY BARBECUE SAUCE
KANSAS CITY, MISSOURI

Carmen Sharp developed this sauce from her grandmother's secret Cajun barbecue sauce recipe. She and her husband, former Kansas City council member John Sharp, first marketed the sauce as "Grandma Richie's Barbecue Sauce." Later they changed the name to Jazzy. Fortunately, when Carmen and John were ready to sell, Lewis P. Bunch of the BBQ Bunch was ready to buy. Jazzy Hot 'n Spicy is tomato-based, smooth, and sweet. The combination of Southern flavors, Cajun spices, and a hint of celery delivers a fiery but tolerable finish. The BBQ Bunch also makes this award-winning sauce in a mild version. Use Jazzy as a finishing or dipping sauce on pork, chicken, beef, or seafood. Put it in your beans and chili.

JO B'S CHILLIUNA HOT MARINADE & DIPPING SAUCE
WARREN, VERMONT

Jo B's Chilliuna is a bridge sauce, connecting east with west and barbecuers with vegetarians. They don't call it a barbecue sauce, but *marinade* and *dipping* are barbecue words, so barbecuers are likely to pick up Jo B's and try it—especially since it is shelved with barbecue sauces. Jo B's Chilliuna demonstrates what soy, fresh ginger, and garlic can do for meat. Although the sauce contains a small amount of vinegar, the flavor of Jo B's Chilliuna is a complete departure from tomato, mustard, or vinegar-based sauces. Try it first as a dipping or sprinkling sauce on chopped barbecued pork, sliced barbecued brisket, or barbecued chicken.

The saltiness from soy sauce, the tartness from fresh ginger and vinegar, the nuttiness from toasted sesame seeds, and the spiciness from fresh chiles will wake up your mouth and put a twist on your favorite barbecued meats. Jo B's also goes well with grilled vegetables and rice.

JUMP INTO AN OPEN GRAVE BBQ SAUCE
MASSAPEQUA, NEW YORK

Jim "Trim" Tabb, of Tryon, North Carolina, has suggested that every barbecuer should choose a "burial sauce." Jump into an Open Grave is a good one to consider. The name suggests that it's hot enough to make you take a flaming leap into the nearest open grave. If you don't use this sauce with respect and moderation, you may *want* to jump. Boiled habañero pepper—a major player in the fiery foods arsenal—is the lead ingredient. The peppers are blended with liquid smoke, honey, malt vinegar, Worcestershire sauce, tomatoes, and pineapple juice in a smooth finishing and dipping sauce that makes you yearn and burn. Instead of yearning for an open grave, however, you'll yearn for more sauce. The burn is persistent and pleasant. There's just enough pineapple juice to impart a brilliant new accent to the habañero flavor. Applause to Big Daddy Jean-Piere Gelinas, and Big Mama Loretta A. Gelinas, for creating this fabulous sauce!

J'S ORIGINAL UPPER MISSISSIPPI BAR-B-QUE SAUCE
MINNEAPOLIS, MINNESOTA

When the late Jay Rosenthal heard that his original recipe hot barbecue sauce had won Best Barbecue Sauce on the Planet at the 1994 American Royal International Barbecue Sauce Contest, he was ecstatic. To the regret of his many friends and business associates, Mr. Rosenthal died a month later from a brain tumor. Fortunately, his partner, Pat Kinney, has continued the business. J's Original Upper Mississippi Bar-B-

Que Sauce has the ideal texture to stick to meat. This smooth, tomato-based sauce is a complex blend of fourteen spices, three types of sweetness, apple cider vinegar, and other flavor enhancers. Upper Mississippi's tangy, sweet, smoky fire is ideal on ribs, beef, pork, chicken, sausage, and grilled vegetables. The fire, from three types of peppers, won't blank your taste buds. In addition to making your meat taste better, Upper Mississippi will add class and distinctiveness to your barbecue beans. The Upper Mississippi Sauce Company also sells the original in mild and medium versions. More treats for fiery eaters are Upper Mississippi's Fire Silk, Cool Jerk, and Hot Salsa-Que.

K-CASS KICKIN'
HOT BAR-B-QUE SAUCE
PLEASANT HILL, MISSOURI

Never underestimate the power of a six-year-old. Had Rich Tuttle Jr. not experimented with sauces and spices on his dinner plate one night, the famous K-Cass Bar-B-Que Sauce would not have been born. It took his parents, Rich and Bunny Tuttle, three full days to duplicate the sauce Rich Jr. had invented on his plate. When they did, a classic was born. The Tuttles and their four children, who serve as the "research and development division," named the sauce K for nearby Kansas City and Cass for Cass County, Missouri, where they live. K-Cass Kickin' Hot Bar-B-Que Sauce is the fiery version of the original sauce. Its tomato-based sweet and spicy Kansas City flavors are embellished with a peppery, Cajun accent. K-Cass has won awards in local, national, and international sauce contests and has helped many barbecue cooking teams win contests. It finishes and dips with the standard variety of barbecued meats and side dishes. The company motto is, "We put a little kick in every bite." Get kicked. You'll love it.

LEGEND DEEP SOUTH BARBECUE SAUCE

CHICAGO, ILLINOIS

Legend Deep South Barbecue Sauce is from the spicier side of Charles Moore's family tradition. Deep South can take you from somber to joyful, without catching your mouth on fire. It is on the gentler side of fiery. Thick, textured with bits of onion and bell peppers, this rich, spicy sauce with a hint of smoke is great for dipping with chicken, beef, pork, and shrimp. It's excellent on grilled burgers too. See the "Mild" section for other Legend sauces.

MAD DOG ULTRA HOT BBQ SAUCE

BOSTON, MASSACHUSETTS

David Ashley, founder and president of Ashley Food Company introduced Mad Dog BBQ Sauce to the barbecue consumer public more than a decade ago. It was an instant hit and has steadily attracted more customers year after year. No wonder the dog on the label with a mischievous gleam in his eye is smiling. I've been a Mad Dog fan since David sent me an extra bottle the first year he entered his award-winning sauce in the American Royal International Barbecue Sauce, Rub, & Baste Contest. Mad Dog hits you up front with a fresh-tasting tomato base laced with hickory smoke, herbs, and secret spices. Mad Dog Ultra Hot puts fire in your mouth and fire in your belly, but, as David says, it's "not overpowering, you can actually taste the sauce through the sizzle." For less fire, get Mad Dog Original or Mad Dog Mild. Mad Dog is great on all of your grilling and barbecuing favorites, including hot dogs.

MAD PEPPER CO.
HOT MOLE-ASSES MADNESS
BBQ SAUCE

MADEIRA BEACH, FLORIDA

Dave and Judith Stone were born with a gift for making culinary magic with peppers. The proof is the exceptional flavor of their Mad Pepper Co. Hot Mole-Asses Madness BBQ Sauce. Judith and Dave make this creative complement to barbecue meat at their El Pass-O Cafe in Madeira Beach, Florida. Hot Mole-Asses Madness is tomato-based, peppered with bell peppers, chipotle, ancho, and cayenne, and embellished with molasses, brown sugar, spices, black pepper, garlic, onion, and balsamic vinegar. The result is a full-flavored, sweet, spicy, fiery nectar with Southwestern overtones. It's great with beef, pork, chicken, and fajitas.

MARTY'S BAR-B-Q
FIRE SAUCE

KANSAS CITY, MISSOURI

Jean Tamburello, maker of Marty's Bar-B-Q Fire Sauce and proprietor of one of Kansas City's most popular barbecue restaurants, makes sure you know there's fire inside her sauce bottle. The attractive label says it in words, flaming graphics, and red lettering. Marty's Fire Sauce will give a fiery message to your palate, too. It has Marty's version of a classic tangy, sweet, peppery, and smoky Kansas City tomato-based sauce, plus Marty's own signature mixture of spices and herbs, including a hint of celery. The grainy texture clings perfectly to your barbecued beef, pork, chicken, turkey, or fish. Try it as a flavor enhancer in barbecue beans and other recipes. Marty's Original Classic Bar-B-Q Sauce gives you Marty's exceptional award-winning flavor, minus the fire.

MRS. DOG'S JAMAICAN JERK MARINADE

GRAND RAPIDS, MICHIGAN

Julie Applegate, creator of this terrific out-of-the-main-stream sauce, credits the Arawak Indians with the development of jerk barbecue. Jerk barbecue is a centuries-old method of preserving, tenderizing, and cooking meat. After being rubbed with jerk sauce, meat is slow-cooked with wood fire from pimento trees.

Do not use Mrs. Dog's Jamaican Jerk as a dipping sauce. It is concentrated. One nine-ounce bottle is enough to flavor and tenderize twenty-four pounds of meat! Straight from the bottle, Mrs. Dog's may overpower your taste buds with salt and fiery peppers. Used as a marinade, baste, or finishing sauce, however, it will give a spicy, fiery, tropical flavor to your barbecued or grilled meats. Jamaican Blue Mountain allspice lends a fragrance and accent that, combined with scotch bonnet peppers, makes Mrs. Dog's extraordinary.

PIGMAN'S BAR-B-QUE AND YE OLDE HAM SHOPPE HOT SAUCE

OUTER BANKS, VIRGINIA

"Easy, baby," says Pigman to the amorous hog licking his bearded cheek on the label of this famous sauce. That's good advice for using Pigman's Bar-B-Que Hot Sauce, too. "Take it easy, but," as Woody Guthrie used to say, "take it." Pigman's Outer Banks, Virginia, hot barbecue sauce is in the Eastern Carolina vinegar and peppers tradition. This one features seven flavorful peppers that will burn you but won't hurt you. Excellent complement to pulled or chopped pork as a finishing sauce. Sprinkle with moderation until you find the level of heat you can tolerate. Pigman also makes a less fiery Regular Sauce, a buttery Grilling Sauce, a sweet and tangy Rib-Roarin' Sauce, and a Rub-A-Dub Meat & Rib Rub.

PRIVATE HARVEST CHIPOTLE BARBEQUE SAUCE

LAKEPORT, CALIFORNIA

Although Private Harvest is presented in a small wine bottle, the only alcohol in this sauce is a touch of beer. The sauce, however, is a gourmet wine for your feasts from the grill or the pit, excellent for finishing or dipping barbecued meats and vegetables. Private Harvest's fresh-tasting, smooth tomato-based sweetness, with a pleasant bite from blended smoked jalapeño peppers, is exceptional.

ROCKIN' ROGER'S SOUL BAR-B-Q SAUCE

GEORGETOWN, CONNECTICUT

Although dressed in the graphics and language of 1950s rock 'n roll, Rockin' Roger's Soul Bar-B-Q Sauce is a serious sauce for today's ribs. The label may attract baby boomers, but the sauce will grab anyone who likes a good condiment on their barbecue. The texture is smooth, with a slight graininess and some bits of pepper. Honey and brown sugar lend a touch of sweetness to Rockin' Roger's, but the zesty power of vinegar and lemon juice are more dominant. Rockin' Roger's secret pepper medley is what makes this an outstanding sauce. The fiery pepper burn is

slow and won't set your mouth on fire. Put Rockin' Roger's on your ribs, your chicken, your pork tenderloin, and your leisure suit—or whatever you're wearing when you're devouring barbecue dipped in Rockin' Roger's.

SANTA FIRE HONEY CHIPOTLE BAR-B-Q SAUCE & MARINADE

SANTA FE, NEW MEXICO

Creative labeling, backed by culinary talent, gives Santa Fire Honey Chipotle an edge over ordinary barbecue sauces. Zesty sweet in a smooth tomato base with bits of onion and garlic, this sauce's fire from smoked jalapeño peppers imparts a perfect finish. Chipotle fire pleasantly lingers as a tingle on your tongue and lips. Santa Fire is an excellent dipping sauce for grilled or barbecued chicken, pork, and beef.

WILBERT H. SCHMITTELS GOURMET BBQ SAUCE
ST. LOUIS, MISSOURI

Habañero peppers and red pepper sauce give the hot version of Wilbert H. Schmittels Gourmet BBQ Sauce an up-front, in-your-mouth wake-up call. The fire doesn't overpower the flavor, however. In the hot or original mild versions, Schmittels's dark, tomato base, with a bouquet of smoke and spices, is loaded with sweet and spicy flavor. The texture is thick and smooth, with bits of onion. The late Wilbert H. Schmittel developed the recipe over fifty years ago. He made it when family and friends gathered. Many people urged Wilbert to sell the sauce, but he was content to keep it in the family. Wilbert did, however, give the recipe to his nephew, Dave Wychel, when Dave asked for it. Dave and Wilbert's son, Randy, have been successfully marketing the sauce in specialty stores for several years. Randy makes and markets Schmittels in the St. Louis, Missouri, metro area, and Dave does the same in North Carolina. Randy perfected the fiery version. He obviously has inherited his dad's culinary talent.

SCOSHI'S DIAMOND BBQ SAUCE
HONOKA'A, HAWAII

"A generous pinch of Aloha," or love, is listed with the ingredients. Love does fantastic magic with the red ripe tomatoes, Worcestershire and pepper sauces, fennel, and other flavor-packed ingredients in this sauce that earns its "diamond" title. Scoshi's Diamond is thick, but your patience when pouring it from the bottle will be rewarded. Scoshi's tomato base is blended with chunky, sweet, complex flavors from a medley of herbs and spices. The pepper finish delivers a pleasant fieriness that is tolerable to people who generally avoid hot.

Scoshi's also makes a Konashire Sauce, which, added to red ripe tomatoes, is the major ingredient of the barbecue sauce. You can also use Scoshi's Blood Mary Mix to make excellent homemade sauces. Thanks to Peter Back and company for chef testing an excellent line of products, flavored with love.

SMOKESTACK LIGHTNING BARBECUE SAUCE

GIBSONIA, PENNSYLVANIA

Smokestack Lightning is peppery and spicy, in a tomato base laced with Worcestershire sauce. The name fits. There's enough fire in this sauce to strike your palate like a bolt of lightning, but you'll let it strike twice and come back for more. Smokestack Lightning is smooth, sticks to meat, and brings out the meat's flavor—a great complement to barbecued beef, pork, and chicken. Use it moderately. Bottled lightning should be handled with care.

STARNES BAR-B-Q SAUCE

PADUCAH, KENTUCKY

Starnes is a simple sauce that makes a simple statement. At the restaurant on Joe Clifton Road in Paducah, loyal patrons and tourists who stop by because they've heard about Starnes have kept them busy since they opened in 1954. Starnes hickory-smoked chopped pork or mutton sandwiches are served between two square slices of white bread, toasted on the outside. Order your sandwich mild and it gets a few shakes of Starnes Bar-B-Q Sauce. Order it hot and a few more shakes of sauce go on. Although Starnes sauce contains some sugar and dextrose, vinegar and hot red pepper do most of the talking. Tomato ketchup and black pepper add accent. Excellent with pork, mutton, chicken, and fish. Starnes also works well as a hot sauce on scrambled eggs, fried potatoes, and a variety of other foods.

TEXAS STAMPEDE HABAÑERO BARBECUE SAUCE

SELMA, TEXAS

Sporting a label the color of ripe habañero peppers, with seven stampeding bison, Texas Stampede grabs your attention. Texas Stampede's tomato ketchup base is thinned with vinegars and lime juice. Brown sugar and molasses thicken the sauce and add a touch of sweetness. Pepper and spice flakes give texture and balance to the sweet and tangy flavors. The fire from habañeros sneaks up on you, but it won't make you stampede for heat relief. Instead, your taste buds will stampede for more. This sauce is best on traditional Texas barbecued beef brisket but is also excellent with chicken, sausage, bologna, and pork ribs.

TWO BUDDIES HOMESTYLE BBQ SAUCE

PORT HUENEME, CALIFORNIA

Patrick and Phil, the two buddies who developed these fantastic sauces, started with Macho Mesquite, born in connection with "BBQ Night" at their Santa Barbara restaurant. The customers loved it. When Macho Mesquite won first place at the Santa Barbara County Fair and the California State Fair, Two Buddies Foods was born. Later, Patrick and Phil developed Hickory Sweet and a Marinade for Santa Barbara Beef.

Macho Mesquite is fired with enough jalapeños to gently jolt your taste buds. The sweet, chunky blend of peppers and secret spices in a tomato base is accented with a generous splash of mesquite smoke. Hickory Sweet carries the same signature flavors of Macho Mesquite, minus the fire from jalapeños, with hickory smoke instead of mesquite. Both sauces are fantastic with all barbecued meats, and with baked beans and meat loaf. The clever labels are the art of Joel Nakamura.

UNCLE DOUGIE'S "WORLD'S MOST DANGEROUS" BARBECUE SAUCE

BARRINGTON, ILLINOIS

Uncle Dougie's upbeat animated labels are irresistible to barbecue sauce collectors. The centerpiece is an uppity rooster with smoke pouring from his mouth. Friendly pigs and bulls also appear on the labels. How dangerous is the fiery Uncle? It's hot enough to tingle your tongue and wet your forehead, but you won't be dialing 911. Smooth, dark, and tomatoey, with flecks of red pepper and herbal tones, Uncle Dougie's "World's Most Dangerous" Barbecue Sauce will perk up your chicken and make your ribs sassy.

For people who want to avoid danger, Uncle Dougie makes a popular Wild-Mild Barbecue Sauce, a "Chicago Style" Chicken Wing Marinade, and Grub-Rub Seasoning.

WING-TIME ORIGINAL BAR-B-QUE SAUCE

DAVIS, CALIFORNIA

As the name and logo suggest, Wing-Time established its fame as a buffalo chicken wing sauce. Wing-Time Buffalo Wing Sauce covers the spectrum from mild to super-hot. Although Wing-Time is based in Davis, California, founder Terry Brown was raised in the buffalo chicken wing country of upstate New York. Wing-Time Original Bar-B-Que Sauce is refreshingly different from traditional tomato-based sauces. The flavor is up front and smooth, with a wholesome, complex blend of Louisiana-style hot sauce, soy sauce, secret spices, and a gentle fiery finish. Of course Wing-Time is great on barbecue chicken—but put it on your ribs and brisket too.

IS YOUR FAVORITE SAUCE MISSING?

For one reason or another, your favorite sauce may not be in the main body of this book. Below I have listed more sauces worthy of your attention. I apologize if your favorite sauce is still missing.

ANCIENT AGE HICKORY BARREL BARBEQUE SAUCE
Frankfort, Kentucky: A sweet and peppery, smooth tomato base, with a bourbon aroma and finish.

ARMADILLO WILLY'S BBQ SAUCE
Los Altos, California: Award-winning tomato-based sauces with a Texas accent and a wonderful jalapeño bite.

ATLANTA BURNING
Newnan, Georgia: A very popular tomato-based sauce fired with habañero peppers.

AUSTIN'S OWN B-B-Q SAUCE
Austin, Texas: A spicy Texas tomato-based sauce from the original Cayton family recipe.

BAD NEWS ALL-PURPOSE SAUCE
Washington, D.C.: Is "Bad News" not an ideal name for a Foggy Bottom sauce? Jim "Bad News" Barnes makes this tangy tomato-based sauce that promises to do something for everything, including barbecue. Jim says his sauce is "Bad News" for all other sauces.

BEAR CREEK SMOKEHOUSE ORIGINAL TEXAS STYLE BARBEQUE SAUCE

Marshall, Texas: Bear Creek has an excellent balance of tomato, with a wink of sweetness and a zesty pepper finish. The hot version, Texas Heatwave, puts a slow burn on your tongue.

BIG DADDY'S BAR-B-Q SAUCES

Des Moines, Iowa: Isaac "Big Daddy" Seymour is known throughout metropolitan Des Moines for his Bahama-style fiery barbecue sauces such as Last Supper Plus, Check-Out Time, and Emergency Room. He also makes mild sauce.

BILL JOHNSON'S BIG APPLE BARBEQUE SAUCE

Glendale, Arizona: Said to be "Arizona's No. 1 selling Barbeque Sauce," this sauce is featured at Bill Johnson's restaurants and was bottled in response to customer demand.

BILLY BLUES BARBECUE SAUCE

San Antonio, Texas: Billy Blues sauces are best known for coffee in tomato-based barbecue sauces.

BISIGNANO'S BARBECUE SAUCE

Des Moines, Iowa: Bisignano's has a choice sweet and tangy chopped-tomato base with an up-front smoke and mellow spice finish. It has been made and served at Chuck's Restaurant since 1956 from a Bisignano family recipe. It's sold in Iowa supermarkets, and for mail order call Linda after 4:30 P.M., 515-244-4104.

BLUE COYOTE HOT PEPPER MUSTARD RELISH

Westbrook, Connecticut: Blue Coyote isn't labeled as a barbecue sauce, but the spicy hot mustard blended with relish is excellent on barbecued and grilled foods.

BOB EVANS FARMS BARBECUE SAUCE

Columbus, Ohio: The thick, sweet, smoky tomato base laced with onion pieces is especially good when served warm, with chicken, beef, and pork.

BOSSE HOGGE SPECIAL BARBEQUE SAUCE

Norfolk, Virginia: Sauces developed by Terry "Bosse Hogge" Grape are for traditional pig-pickin' barbecue. They're also good on beef, chicken, game, seafood, and vegetables.

BOURBON "Q"
Pee Wee Valley, Kentucky: Bourbon-based award winner from the Kentucky Cookout Company, for dipping, marinating, or basting.

BUFFALO WHIZ PRIMO BEER BARBEQUE SAUCE
Shawnee Mission, Kansas: Sweet and smooth with chopped onion, smoke, beer, and spices, Buffalo Whiz looks like a novelty but tastes like serious sauce. From Puddle Jumpers, appropriately.

BULL HEAD BARBECUE SAUCE
Taiwan, Republic of China: A famous Chinese barbecue sauce made of brill fish, soybean oil, garlic, chile pepper, and dried shrimp. Recommended for beef, pork, chicken, and sea slugs.

BUSHA BROWN'S SPICY JERK SAUCE
Spanish Town, Jamaica, West Indies: Busha Brown's is a thin, dark, smooth, fiery nectar with fruity overtones and tangy pepper fire finish. Although it is made for jerk cooking, I like to use it as a table sauce for sprinkling on my barbecue.

CAFE SERRANOS CHIPOTLE BARBEQUE SAUCE
Austin, Texas: Smoked jalapeño peppers lend signature to this Texas tomato-based sauce.

CAFE TATTOO
Baltimore, Maryland: Unfortunately, Elayne and Rick Catalano's splendiferous barbecue sauces, marinades, and rubs are made locally in small batches. Fortunately, you can go to Baltimore and meet Rick and Elayne and ask them to sell you some Baltimore Belly Burner or Black Jack Barbecue Sauce or Rick's Radical Rub or any number of other award-winning Elayne/Rick creations. Black Jack, featuring a magic measure of Jack Daniel's sour mash whiskey, is my favorite. For a tattoo, go upstairs to see Elayne.

THE CAJUN GRILL BAR-B-QUE SAUCE
Lafayette, Louisiana: A Southern Louisiana basting or finishing sauce, in a mustard and soybean oil base, with a touch of tomato paste, Cajun spices, and a cayenne pepper-bite finish. Follow the directions on the label for some great Cajun chicken.

CALVERT'S CHESAPEAKE BAY BBQ & BRUSH ON
El Paso, Texas: Texas?! With a big crab on the label and Chesapeake Bay in the name? Yep. It's a familiar tomato base with an

East Coast accent. Twelve traditional old bay herbs and spices make the difference, giving your palate a spice kick in the tongue, with a lingering pepper tickle. Calvert's is an excellent finishing and dipping sauce for ribs, pork shoulder, and chicken.

CAROLINA TREET
Wilmington, North Carolina: Carolina Treet is a regionally popular vinegar-based "cooking sauce" thickened with wheat flour and xanthan gum and flavored with garlic, onion, and spices. I like it as a finishing and dipping sauce.

CATTLEMEN'S BARBECUE SAUCE
Wayne, New Jersey: Cattlemen's is sold primarily to restaurants, one of the most popular brands in the industry. They sell an excellent variety of tomato-based barbecue sauces.

CHARLIE ROBINSON'S BARBECUE SAUCE
Oak Park, Illinois: This is a great finishing and dipping sauce, just right for sticking to ribs. The smooth, sweet, spicy tomato base has a Mississippi tanginess at the finish. Also comes in Hot and Classic Brown Sugar.

COOKSHACK SPICY BARBECUE SAUCE
Ponca City, Oklahoma: Cookshack makes an excellent variety of dry spice mixes for barbecued meats. In 1990, they started bottling and marketing their barbecue sauce. Cookshack's award-winning flavor is sweet and spicy in a tomato base, with a hint of smoke.

COUNTRY BOB'S ALL-PURPOSE SAUCE
Centralia, Illinois: Country Bob's has a sweet and tangy balance with a Worcestershire sauce finish. Great on steaks and lots more.

COWPOKE CUISINE BUCKIN' BARBECUE
Bellvue, Colorado: This is a thin, tangy/sweet tomato-based sauce with spices and hickory smoke. Manufactured by Brother Mel's Foods for the Stove Prairie Collection.

THE CREATIVE CHEF RASPBERRY JALAPEÑO GOURMET SAUCE
Belton, Missouri: Fred Fatino deserves a barbecue Oscar for creating this perfect balance of fresh raspberries, sugar, jalapeño peppers, vinegar, salt, and spices. Although not

labeled as a barbecue sauce, it's a repeat performer with barbecue chicken and pork at my house.

DIAMOND JIM'S GOURMET DIAMOND MINE BAR-B-Q SAUCE

Flower Mound, Texas: Chunks of onion, garlic, and herbs dance in a spicy, tangy tomato ketchup laced with olive oil and a touch of fennel, making this sauce a great baste on beef, pork, and chicken.

DICKEY'S BARBECUE SAUCE

Dallas, Texas: Tomato-based Texas sauce sold at Dickey's restaurants and local stores since 1941.

SAM DILLARD'S BAR-B-Q SAUCE

Durham, North Carolina: Tomato-based, with an accent of vinegar and spices.

DIXIE & NIKITA'S WICKED AWESOME BARBECUE SAUCE

Boston, Massachusetts: An award-winning spicy tomato-based sauce from Boston. Some of the profits are donated to charity.

DOT JONES COCONUT GROVE HOT & SPICY BARBEQUE SAUCE

Coconut Grove, Florida: Hot peppers and vinegar blended with complementary spices, tomato paste, and other seasonings put an exceptionally good tangy/fiery Dot Jones signature on your barbecue.

DREAMLAND BAR-B-Q SAUCE

Tuscaloosa, Alabama: World-famous spiced and sweetened tomato-based sauce with a secret zing.

ELDER HARRIS BAR-B-QUE SAUCE

Fort Lauderdale, Florida: This famous sauce made from spiced and herbed tomato juice, mustard, and lemon juice is reserved for "distinguished people" who eat ribs at All People's Bar-B-Que.

ENRICO'S BARBECUE SAUCE

Syracuse, New York: A thick, mild, tomato paste base seasoned with apple cider vinegar, spices, lemon juice, onion powder, garlic powder, and a taste of honey.

THE FEED STORE B-B-Q SAUCE

Colorado City, Texas: Rusty Fleming makes a tomato-based sauce in small batches, the old-fashioned way.

GAYLE'S EXTRA SASSY BARBEQUE SAUCE

Beverly Hills, California: Thick, tomatoey, and spicy, with a sassy, fiery bite and a black pepper finish. Mop Gayle's on chicken, brisket, or veggies.

GERWER TEX-MEX HICKORY B.B.Q. SAUCE

Plano, Texas: A tomato-based "Taste of the Old West" from Gerwer Foods.

RAY "RED" GILL'S RAZORBACK BARBECUE SAUCE

Blytheville, Arkansas: Mr. Ray "Red" Gill knows how to cook barbecue. He also knows how to build a plain, simple sauce that marries perfectly with barbecued meat. Tomato, vinegar, brown sugar, and a variety of spices are mixed in secret proportions to give this sauce a great balance between sweet, tangy, and spicy. Wild boar, domestic boar, chicken, and beef take well to Razorback Barbecue Sauce.

GIOVANNI'S BARBECUE SAUCE

Berwyn, Illinois: Tom Ferguson uses this tomato-based sauce in his popular Chicago restaurant and at rib competitions in other cities. His busy restaurant and his many ribbons, trophies, and plaques testify to the merits of the sauce.

GOYA MOJO CRIOLLO SPANISH BAR-B-Q SAUCE

Secaucus, New Jersey: Citrus juices, garlic, onion, and spices make up this excellent marinade, mop, and finishing sauce for pork and chicken.

GOYA NARANJA AGRIA

Secaucus, New Jersey: This marinade, mop, and finishing sauce—made from concentrated Seville orange juice—adds a citrus twist to grilled or barbecued pork, chicken, and beef.

GRAHAM'S BARBEQUE SAUCE

Springfield, Missouri: This vinegar-based sauce, with tomato ketcup, salt, secret spices, and sugar, is fabulous for dipping or basting. The vinegar tanginess is bolstered with a complex balance of spicy sweetness. Graham's is an exceptional complement to pulled pork and pork ribs.

GUADALUPE, THE BARBEQUE SAUCE

New Braunfels, Texas: The Guadalupe Smoked Meat Company Restaurant serves their dipping sauce warm. The spicy, smooth tomato base with a Worcestershire finish is a winner on brisket, smoked sausage, chicken, and bologna.

HARD ROCK CAFE WATERMELON B-B-Q SAUCE

Los Angeles, California, and elsewhere: The only drawback to this creative blend of fresh watermelon, tomato, chile peppers, garlic, Tabasco, vinegar, and spices is that it has to be kept refrigerated—that is, if you have any left when you've devoured a slab of ribs.

HARRY AND DAVID'S ORIGINAL OREGON TRAIL SAUCE

Medford, Oregon: An excellent tomato-based all-purpose barbecue sauce and more, it measures up to Harry and David's high standards for quality.

THE HAWG PEN

Prairie Village, Kansas: Hawg Pen is a smooth and spicy tomato-based finishing and dipping sauce from a championship barbecue cooking team.

HAYWARD'S PIT BARBECUE SAUCE

Overland Park, Kansas: This smooth, sweet, spicy tomato-based sauce with a hint of cumin and a peppery finish enhances the flavor of thousands of pounds of pit barbecue prepared by Hayward Spears, his family, and associates each week. Sold in supermarkets or at the restaurant.

HEINZ B-B-Q SAUCE

Pittsburgh, Pennsylvania: Popular tomato-based sauce widely available in several varieties.

JOHN HENRY'S EAST TEXAS BARBECUE SAUCE

Houston, Texas: The original flavor is a tomato-based sauce with a chile seasonings accent and a hint of smoke.

HUNT'S BARBECUE SAUCE

Fullerton, California: Another industry giant that offers a variety of widely available tomato-based barbecue sauces.

JACKIE'S OKLAHOMA–STYLE BARBECUE SAUCE

Oakland, California: Jackie's is a thick, tomato-based combination of brown sugar sweetness, cider vinegar tanginess, and a kiss of smoke that will strike a familiar chord with Oklahomans and Southwesterners.

JANE'S BEST BARBEQUE SAUCE
Bruce, Wisconsin: Jane's is an all-natural, fresh, tomato-based gourmet sauce. It is smooth and lightly spiced with, as Jane says, "a touch above the usual" and a hint of hickory smoke.

JONESY'S SMOKY RIB & WING BAR-B-QUE SAUCE
North East, Pennsylvania: Oh so sweet and oh so good, this sauce has a very smooth sweetened tomato base with a touch of vinegar, spices, hickory smoke, and lemon juice.

KAUI NATURALS ISLAND GRILLE SAUCE
Hanalei, Hawaii: Kaui is a thick, spicy blend of canola oil with a refreshing tropical medley of tomatillos, tomato, vinegar, soy sauce, lime juice, jalapeños, ginger, Dijon mustard, and sea salt, sweetened with papaya, turbinado sugar, molasses, and honey. The gentle burn from jalapeños is as comforting as a tropical sun.

KC BARON OF BARBECUE
Shawnee Mission, Kansas: Paul Kirk, Ph.B., the Baron of Barbecue, is a genius with sauces and seasonings. He makes a variety of his own and private label award-winning sauces.

KEY WEST'S S.O.B. B-B-Q SAUCE
Deland, Florida: Caribbean-inspired spicy, fiery "Sauces of the Border."

KOZLOWSKI FARMS CALIFORNIA-STYLE BARBECUE SAUCE
Forestville, California: An excellent tomato-based sauce seasoned with the bounty of California harvests, including Cabernet Sauvignon.

LALLY'S CLASSIC BLEND BARBECUE SAUCE
LeMars, Iowa: A sweet, smooth, lightly spiced tomato base with a tangy finish and smoky accent.

LEHMANN FARMS BIG JAKE'S NORTH WOODS STYLE BBQ SAUCE
Spring Park, Minnesota: Big Jake's has a honey-sweet up-front flavor, with a tangy, spicy, finish, in a thick tomato base. This

sauce will stick to your ribs and liven up your shoulder or brisket. Available in original flavor and several variations.

LLOYD'S ORIGINAL BARBEQUE SAUCE
St. Paul, Minnesota: A smooth, thick, smoky, sweet tomato base with a tangy, spicy pepper finish. Sold only in stores. Call Lloyd's toll-free number to find out who sells it near you.

LUCKY LUKE'S BAR-B-Q DIPPING SAUCE
La Honda, California: The thick, tomato base with a chile pepper/cloves/herbal accent leaves a lingering touch of gentle fire on your lips and palate.

LULING CITY MARKET BAR-B-QUE SAUCE
Houston, Texas: A tangy and peppery sauce, with ketchup/vinegar accents, a little bit of sugar, some secret spices, and turmeric, Luling's is one of my all-time favorite barbecue sauces. Luling's on a barbecued beef sandwich is one step short of heaven.

LUZIANNE CAJUN BARBECUE SAUCE
New Orleans, Louisiana: Pickle vinegar and scattered Cajun spices blended with tomato paste and mustard make this sauce ideal for chopped pork, po' boys, chicken, and seafood.

MAKER'S MARK BOURBON GOURMET SAUCE
Loretto, Kentucky: Tomato-based sauce with herbs, spices, and the famous Kentucky bourbon.

MANSMITH'S GOURMET CONCENTRATED BARBECUE PASTE
San Juan Bautista, California: Jon Mansmith makes a creative selection of award-winning barbecue and grilling pastes for dilution with water, juices, beer, wine, or other liquids of your choice.

MARK'S FEED STORE
Louisville, Kentucky: Mark Erwin has developed two award-winning sauces for his growing chain of Mark's Feed Store Barbecue Restaurants. Mark's original vinegar and mustard Southern-style sauce and his more recent sweet, tomato-based sauce are sold at his restaurants and in retail stores.

MCCLARD'S BAR-B-Q SAUCE
Hot Springs, Arkansas: This tangy tomato-based classic has

been pleasing customers since Alex and Gladys McClard opened their famous restaurant in 1928. Lemon juice puts pucker on your lips and pleasure on your pork. It's also fabulous on cantaloupe, with or without prosciutto.

MELINDA'S ORIGINAL HABANERO BARBECUE SAUCE
New Orleans, Louisiana: A seasoned tomato-based sauce fired with habañero peppers.

MRS. RENFRO'S BARBECUE SAUCE
Fort Worth, Texas: Thin, smooth, tomato-based, Texas spicy and tangy, Mrs. Renfro's has been the mild or hot barbecue sauce of choice for several generations of Southwesterners.

MUIR GLEN ORGANIC GRILL CHEF BARBECUE SAUCE
Sacramento, California: A touch of smoke up front and at the finish, with sweet spiciness and a hint of tanginess makes Organic Grill Chef a versatile finishing and dipping sauce for all occasions.

NOH HAWAIIAN BAR-B-Q SAUCE
Honolulu, Hawaii: A sweet tomato-based sauce for great Hawaiian ribs and more.

OASIS EXTRA THICK SWEET 'N' SASSY BBQ SAUCE
Austin, Texas: Molasses and honey make it sweet. Fiery peppers make it sassy. A lemon juice finish lends a little pucker to your lips. Best on chicken, pork, and shrimp.

OINK, CACKLE AND MOO BBQ SAUCE
Tullahoma, Tennessee: Tomato-based sauces with the down-home flavors of great Tennessee cooking.

OPEN PIT ORIGINAL BARBECUE SAUCE
Camden, New Jersey: A very smooth, tangy tomato base with pepper bite, Open Pit has been a staple as is, or with added onion, pepper, or other ingredients, favored by backyard pit-masters for over forty years.

ORANGE BLOSSOM SPECIAL BARBECUE SAUCE
Orlando, Florida: Fred and Linda Burnett make small quantities of this fabulous spicy orange juice-based sauce and sell them at barbecue cooking contests.

PAPA DON'S BARBEQUE SAUCE
Maple Plain, Minnesota: Papa Don's orange juice base delivers a smooth, sweet, smoky blast of flavor with a spicy, tangy lemon juice finish. Here's more proof that barbecue sauce excellence can go beyond tomato. Papa Don's is versatile enough to complement your entire repertoire of barbecued and grilled foods.

PAPA SPARROW'S JERK SAUCE
Calgary, Canada: Thick and grainy, with a fruity bouquet. Papa Sparrow's complex blend of habañero peppers, scallions, lemon juice, fresh garlic, ginger, secret spices, and herbs has an up-front burn and a finish hinting of clove or allspice. Sam Shivji, the creator of this wonderful sauce, insists on using only the best ingredients. You'll appreciate the result.

PERSIMMON HILL BERRY FARM BBQ SAUCES
Lampe, Missouri: Persimmon Hill makes award-winning smooth, tomato-based sauces, with splendid sweetness from berries complemented with secret spices in raspberry, blueberry, and more flavors.

PROSPECTOR'S CHOICE ORIGINAL BAR-B-QUE SAUCE
Tombstone, Arizona: A portion of money from the sale of Prospector's Choice Original Bar-B-Que Sauce supports the upkeep and restoration of Tombstone, Arizona, a late-nineteenth-century silver town. Tombstone is also the site of a famous gunfight at the O.K. Corral. Named in honor of the prospectors who made Tombstone famous, this sweet, smoky, flavorful tomato-based sauce with a gentle hit of chipotle peppers is excellent as a dipping sauce with beef, chicken, pork shoulder, ribs, and beans.

QUE QUEENS LOVE POTION FOR THE SWINE
Kansas City, Missouri: A limited-edition barbecue sauce made by Kansas City's famous Que Queens for the Harvesters.

RASTA JOE'S B-B-Q
Plymouth, Indiana: Tomato-based, with fresh green peppers, spices, and much more—including Jamaican rum—Rasta Joe's is a repeat winner at rib-cooking contests.

RED HOT & BLUE
Arlington, Virginia: Headquartered in Virginia and spreading

across America via franchises, the Red Hot & Blue Memphis Pit Bar-B-Que restaurant chain bottles its own version of liquid red Memphis mops in Hoochie Coochie Hot and Mojo Mild.

ROBBS RIBBS SOUTHWESTERN BBQ SAUCE

Albuquerque, New Mexico: This smooth, complex blend of beer, molasses, lemon juice, fresh onion, chile pepper, and secret spices in a tomato base is enhanced with a perfect measure of fire in the Habañero Hot version. Robbs will wake up your ribs with sweet, tangy, spicy fire and a Southwestern accent.

ROCKY MOUNTAIN

Redmond, Oregon: An award-winning variety of excellent tomato-based and fruit-based barbecue sauces.

ROSEDALE BARBEQUE

Kansas City, Kansas: There are at least eleven Kansas City barbecue sauces with flavors that echo the Rosedale taste. No coincidence, since at least that many KC pitmasters got their training on the job at this oldest continuously operated barbecue restaurant in the city. There's only one Rosedale sauce—red, tomato-based, balanced between sweet and tangy, with an allspice finish.

RUDY'S COUNTRY BAR-B-Q SAUCE

Leon Springs, Texas: The fingerprints and humorous remarks on the bottle may mislead you into thinking this is merely a novelty sauce. It is serious Texas tangy/spicy tomato-based bodacious barbecue sauce.

SAMSON'S

Greensboro, North Carolina: A great sauce made with vinegar, pepper, and spices and aged in wood; called the "King of Sauces."

SAUCEMASTERS OLD KC BARBEQUE SAUCE

Kansas City, Missouri: A tomato-based award-winning spicy mild sauce, with chopped onions and an excellent balance of flavors.

SCORNED WOMAN FIERY BARBEQUE SAUCE

Atlanta, Georgia: Longtime fans of Scorned Woman Hot Sauce will be delighted to pour her pit sauce on their barbecue. Her fury whaps your mouth, but her sweet, spicy, smoky disposition, with a hint of lemon juice, will bring you back for more. Sissies may scorn her, but all others will keep her in the family.

SCOTT'S RED HOT BARBECUE SAUCE
Goldsboro, North Carolina: An excellent blend of vinegar, salt, peppers, and spices for authentic old South barbecued chicken or pork with a zesty touch of fire.

SELMON BROTHERS BAR-B-QUE SAUCE
Norman, Oklahoma: The Selmon brothers—Dewey, Lucious, and Lee Roy—were all-American football stars at the University of Oklahoma in the mid-1970s, when the Sooners enjoyed a reputation as gridiron godzillas. Today the Selmon brothers are famous for their barbecue sauce. Their old family recipe sauce is built on a sweet tomato base with secret spices and traditional barbecue sauce spices such as cumin and Worcestershire sauce. A hint of mustard, onion, garlic, hot pepper, and vinegar round out the flavor and give it holding power on your palate. Thick enough to stick to meat.

SMOKEHEAD ZESTY BARBEQUE SAUCE
St. Joseph, Missouri: David Arthur makes this thick, smooth, sweet, tomato-based sauce with a spicy, peppery finish.

SNYDER'S FAMOUS BOSS BBQ SAUCE
Yukon, Oklahoma: Richly flavored, thick and spicy in a tomato base, Boss puts a touch of smoky sweetness with a chili powder accent on your brisket, chicken, sausage, bologna, and ribs.

SPICY JONES TEXAS GRILLING
AND DIPPING SAUCE
Houston, Texas: I like Texas. I like spicy. And I like Spicy Jones. Smooth, tomato-based, with tiny chunks of onion, Spicy Jones delivers a pleasing, complex blend of chili pepper, cloves, Worcestershire sauce, and other flavors with a smoky finish.

SPRAYBERRY'S BARBEQUE SAUCE
Newnan, Georgia: A tomato-based spicy tangy-sweet Georgia classic.

THE STACK'S PRIVATE STOCK
Martin City, Missouri: A delicious sweet tomato-based sauce with a peppery finish, from one of Kansas City's most popular barbecue restaurants.

STONEWALL CHILI PEPPER CO. THREE RED ROOSTERS HOT 'N PEACHY TOPPING

Stonewall, Texas: This heavenly nectar with a cocky attitude is made by gifted saucemeister Jeff Campbell for three red roosters restaurant in Ft. Lauderdale, Florida. Although Jeff doesn't call it a barbecue or grill sauce, it is a stellar performer as either. The sugared sweetness of genuine Stonewall Texas peaches, combined with red jalapeños, is one of my favorite complements to grilled chicken breast and pulled pork.

STUBBY'S BAR-B-Q SAUCE

Hot Springs, Arkansas: An aggressive concoction of spiced tomato ketcup and vinegar, Stubby's sauce has complemented tons of hickory-smoked pork and beef purchased by throngs of satisfied Stubby's Hik-Ry Pit Bar-B-Q customers.

SUMSAY BARBECUE SAUCES

Seattle, Washington: Brian Koba's culinary genius and pitmaster excellence can be tasted in every bottle of his fabulous fusion barbecue sauces, which successfully wed combinations of American and Pacific Rim flavors.

SUTPHEN'S BAR-B-Q BBQ SAUCE

Amarillo, Texas: Joey Sutphen has fed thousands of happy customers from all over the country for years. His smooth, Texas-style sauce with a peppery finish is great on barbecued brisket.

SWEET BABY RAY'S BARBECUE SAUCE

Elmwood Park, Illinois: Ray's sauce is sweet indeed, but it's not a baby sauce. Ray's adult formula delivers a spicy bite from peppers, a touch of mesquite smoke, and a tangy vinegar and pineapple accent.

A TASTE OF TEXAS HICKORY BARBECUE SAUCE

Stephenville, Texas: A tomato-based sauce for chuckwagon barbecues.

TEXAS BEST BARBECUE SAUCE

Columbus, Ohio: This very smooth, medium-thick sweet tomato base, gently spiced, with a touch of Texas tanginess is named after company founder Alen Smith's home state. Alen got the recipe from his great aunt Ruby. His great uncle George developed the recipe in 1933. Distributed by T. Marzetti Company.

TEXAS HOSPITALITY SASSY JALAPEÑO BARBECUE SAUCE

Houston, Texas: Two parts sassy-spicy black pepper and bite-your-mouth jalapeño pepper. The combo, in a tomato base with complementary spices and a touch of sweetness, is Texas hospitable to beef, chicken, pork, and sausage.

TIM & TODD'S EXCELLENT BARBEQUE SAUCE

Lee's Summit, Missouri: Tim & Todd's earns the "excellent" designation with a smooth, tomato-based, sweet and spicy, hickory smoke combination. The complex spice combo eases you into borderline fieriness with a Cajun spice, black pepper, and red pepper finish.

UBON'S BAR-B-Q DIPPING SAUCE

Yahoo City, Mississippi: Ubon Roark developed this dark, smooth, sweet, and spicy tomato-based Mississippi masterpiece years ago, and it continues as a Roark family tradition today.

UNCLE SPUNKEY'S BBQ BLAST

Virginia Beach, Virginia: Tomato ketchup serves as an excellent base for the Uncle's special blend of spices, with a hint of bourbon, lemon juice, hot sauce, and a smoky, peppery finish.

VIRGIN ISLANDS FINEST MARINADE & MEAT SAUCE

U.S. Virgin Islands: A fantastic soy sauce-based marinade and table sauce seasoned with vinegar, onions, ginger, herbs, spices, and peppers.

WALKER'S WOOD JAMAICAN JERK BAR-B-QUE SAUCE

St. Ann, Jamaica, West Indies: Your search for a sweet jerk sauce ends here. Your reward is a thick, spicy, banana base with a jerk fiery finish. This sauce can be used as jerk sauce or table sauce with chicken, pork, beef, and seafood.

W. B. WILLIAMS PEACH BAR-B-Q SAUCE

Austin, Texas: The W. B. Williams recipe marries tomato with peaches, spices, vinegar, and a touch of jalapeño to complement your barbecue with a refreshing salsa accent. Also great as a tortilla chip dip.

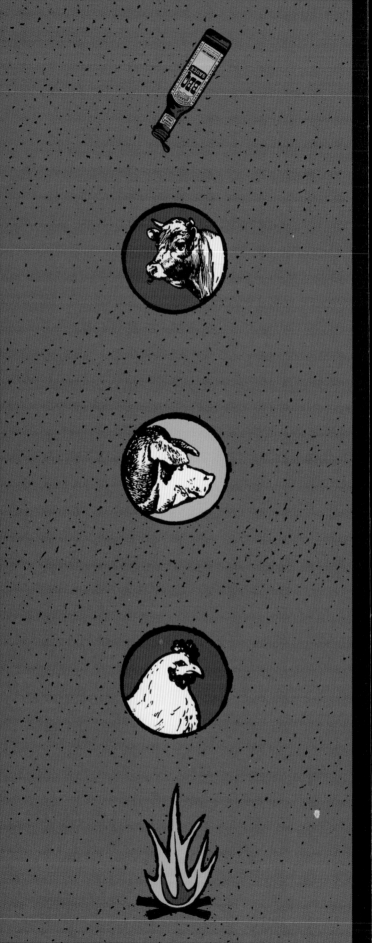

PART TWO
RECIPES

FIERY THAI PEANUT CHIP DIP
SERVES 5

Jeff Sanders, father of Roadhouse Bar-B-Que Sauce, gave me this recipe. It's simple and delicious. If you don't like hot food, substitute Roadhouse mild sauce.

Jeff says you can convert this dip into dinner by adding a splash of fish sauce (available at Asian markets); diced vegetables; shredded chicken, beef, or pork; and hot, cooked, rice noodles.

$\frac{3}{4}$ **cup Roadhouse Hot & Spicy Bar-B-Que Sauce**
$\frac{1}{2}$ **cup creamy peanut butter (regular or reduced fat)**

Mix the sauce and peanut butter in a small bowl until smooth. Serve at room temperature with corn chips, potato chips, tortilla chips, or crackers.

KC BARON'S BARBECUE BEANS
SERVES 8

2 strips thick bacon
1 medium white or yellow onion, chopped
1 red or green bell pepper, chopped
5 15-ounce cans pork and beans, drained and rinsed
2 cups chopped barbecued brisket, burnt ends,
    or rib pieces
1 $\frac{1}{2}$ cups tomato-based barbecue sauce
$\frac{1}{3}$ cup mustard-based barbecue sauce,
    or prepared mustard
1 tablespoon brown sugar
Water or beer, for thinning

Fry the bacon and set it aside. Sauté the onion and the bell pepper in the bacon grease until tender.

Put the beans, onion, peppers, crumbled bacon, barbecued meat, barbecue sauces, and brown sugar in a ceramic casserole. Thin with water or beer, as needed. Smoke (see page 127) the beans, uncovered, for 3 hours at 225°, or add $\frac{1}{4}$ teaspoon liquid hickory smoke and bake in an oven, uncovered, for four hours at 225°. Stir occasionally during cooking.

This recipe is adapted from a discussion with Paul Kirk, Kansas City baron of barbecue, several years ago when we were barbecuing ribs at the Saddle and Sirloin Club for sale at the American Royal Barbecue.

You can experiment with many variations of this basic recipe. Many sauces in this book will work with these beans. Note the ones you like best. You'll be famous among your friends for making the best barbecue beans they've ever tasted.

NOTE: Remember to rinse the beans. This makes a qualitative difference in the flavor.

HOW TO SMOKE

The barbecue method of cooking is simple. Use the following principles for best results:

- Use oak, hickory, pecan, mesquite, alder, apple, maple, or peach for smoke. Other hardwoods may be suitable; avoid pine.
- Wood chips should be soaked in water for at least 1 hour, then drained before being placed on hot coals. Chunks needn't be soaked.
- Arrange 4 pounds of charcoal briquettes so that the food will not sit directly above the hot coals during cooking. If you have a cooker with an external firebox, build your fire in the firebox, not the cooking pit. This method assures that the smoke flavor in the food will be from wood smoke instead of burning grease.
- Light the briquettes and let them burn until covered with gray ash.
- Put wood chips or wood chunks directly atop the hot coals.
- Put the grill rack in the pit, and put the food on the end opposite the coals.
- Cover the pit with the lid and adjust temperature using the air vents. The temperature will rise with more air, and lower with less. I use a candy thermometer in the lid air vent of my kettle-style cooker to monitor the temperature.
- Add coals as necessary. You lose heat and lengthen the cooking time when you lift the lid. Hourly monitoring is sufficient.
- The general rule of the barbecue method of cooking is "slow and low." Slow refers to time. A slab of ribs can take 4 to 6 hours; a brisket, up to 12 or more hours. Low refers to tem-

perature. Most barbecuers maintain a temperature range of 225° to 280°. Grilling, by contrast, is "hot and fast."

See the "Books about Sauce and BBQ" section of this book for some good books on how to smoke.

BEER BUTT CHICKEN

SERVES 4

Who first got the idea for this method of barbecuing chicken? Some say it was Hank Lumpkin of Topeka. Once the idea caught on, however, it spread like prairie fire through the barbecue buddies network. I owe Mike Cannon, "Mayor of the *Memphis In May Barbecue*," for telling me about it.

1 medium fryer, about 3 pounds
12-ounce can of beer

In a kettle cooker (for example, a Weber), place 25 to 30 charcoal briquettes on one side of the "pit." Ignite. Meanwhile, soak three cups of pecan, hickory, peach, or cherry wood chips in water.

Rinse a medium fryer, open a 12-ounce can of beer, (or a 16-ounce can for a larger bird). Take a sip of beer and insert the full can in the chicken cavity, with the can right-side up to avoid spilling beer.

Drain the chips and put them on the coals. Quickly put the grate in place. Put the chicken upright on the grate, opposite the coals, and put the lid on the cooker. Sometimes it's tricky to make the chicken stay upright. Be patient.

Stick a candy thermometer through the cover vent to monitor the temperature. Adjust the bottom vents to attain a temperature of about 225°. Leave the lid on for 2 hours; there should be enough heat in the briquettes to last that long.

The chicken will feel tender and the juices will run clear (no pink liquid) when the chicken is done. Remove the beer can and pour the unevaporated beer in your garden.

Serve the chicken with your favorite barbecue sauces.

CAJUN CHICKEN BATISTE, WITH DAVE'S DIRTY RICE & CLETE'S WHAP YER MOUTH RED BEANS

The following recipes are inspired by a series of books written by James Lee Burke. The books feature a law enforcement officer, Dave Robicheaux, who lives and works in the vicinity of New Iberia, Louisiana.

In addition to his gift for telling compelling stories that pull you into the action, James Lee Burke can describe aromas of places and people with an endless, creative variety of metaphors.

CAJUN CHICKEN BATISTE

SERVES 4

1 medium chicken, about 3 pounds, cut in half

Marinate the chicken overnight in a refrigerator with a 16-ounce jar of McIlhenny Farms Bar-B-Que Sauce.

Soak hardwood oak or pecan chips in water.

Assemble about 30 hardwood briquettes on one end of your barbecue drum or kettle cooker; light and let burn until covered with gray ash.

Drain the water off the chips and put the wet chips on the hot coals.

Put the chicken on the grate, opposite the charcoal, set aside the remaining sauce in the refrigerator, and barbecue the chicken in a covered cooker at 250° for 1 hour. After 1 hour, move the chicken to an 18-inch square sheet of heavy duty aluminum foil, and wrap the chicken in the foil. Before wrapping, pour the remaining sauce on the chicken pieces. Cook for another hour or more until tender and the juices run clear (no pink liquid). Add more charcoal during the cooking process as needed.

If you wish, you can cook the chicken according to the directions on the McIlhenny Farms Bar-B-Que Sauce label instead of using the method above.

Serve Static's Sweet & Sassy or Chunky Onion as a dipping sauce on the side.

Cajun Chicken tastes like a spicy, bodacious, brass band medley of southern Louisiana flavors. It smells like chicken.

DIRTY RICE

SERVES 4

1 ½ cups long grain white enriched rice (cook & refrigerate overnight)
3 cups water
½ lb. fresh chicken livers
1 medium red onion, chopped
1 green bell pepper, chopped
½ cup roasted red bell pepper
1 cup Dr. Pepper
1 tablespoon All Cajun Pee Wee's Green Spiced Pepper Sauce or Cajun Chef Green Pepper Sauce or Louisiana Brand Green Pepper Sauce. If you can't find any of these, use your favorite red pepper sauce.
Salt & pepper to taste

The night before, combine rice and water in a lidded stainless steel pan. Bring water to a boil; reduce to simmer for 20 minutes. Remove from fire. Let sit until it reaches room temperature, then refrigerate.

Place chicken livers on an 18-inch square piece of heavy duty aluminum foil. Put the foil and livers in a barbecue pit and smoke with pecan wood for one hour at 250°.

Or: boil chicken livers in water until done.
Or: bake chicken livers at 275° for 40 minutes.

Combine all ingredients and heat in an oven at 250° until hot.

Serve warm with All Cajun Bruci's Blend Zydeco Seasoning, or your favorite brand of Cajun seasoning, on the side. Your guests can season to fit their invidual taste.

WHAP YER MOUTH RED BEANS

SERVES 4

2 15-ounce cans red beans, rinsed and drained
$^3/_4$ pound chicken andouille sausages, fried, grilled,
    or smoked
$^1/_2$ cup Dixie Beer or your favorite pilsner
Salt and pepper to taste
Enough All Cajun Andre's Rouge, or Tabasco Hot
    Sauce, or Louisiana Hot Sauce, or Red Devil
    Hot Sauce, or your favorite hot barbecue sauce,
    to whap your mouth

Combine the ingredients in a pan and simmer for 20 minutes, adding more beer or water as necessary. Quick, easy, and good.

POSSUM TROT FLORENTINE STEAK

SERVES 4

Chef Giancarlo Gianelli, innkeeper, poet, Barbecue Baron of Tuscany, and owner of Posto di Ristoro a Tocchi, told me how to hay-smoke and grill a famous Chianana T-bone Florentine steak.

Steak is a Kansas City tradition that goes as far back as frontier times when the city was a wagons westward gateway town called Possum Trot.

The following recipe will yield one of the best steaks you have ever eaten. Do not use steak sauce, barbecue sauce, grill sauce, or marinade with your first bites of this steak. A light sprinkle of salt, pepper, or extra virgin olive oil is enough. Try the steak in its primal form before applying your favorite barbecue or steak sauces.

3 1-pound choice Kansas City Strip beefsteaks,
    cut 3 inches thick
Sea salt or kosher salt to taste
Extra virgin olive oil to taste
Freshly ground black pepper
Fresh lemon wedges as garnish

Spread a $^1/_2$-gallon bucket full of clean, pesticide-free prairie hay or wheat straw on a platter and put the steaks on the hay.

Lightly sprinkle the steaks with salt and let them reach room temperature, about 30 minutes.

Light hardwood charcoal (not charcoal briquettes) and a 12 by 6-inch chunk of oak in your grill about twenty minutes before you're ready to grill the steaks.

Set aside the hay and grill the steaks about 3 minutes on each side.

Lift the grate from the fire and carefully drop the hay on the fire. Quickly return the steak-laden grate to its place above the fire. Let both sides of the steak absorb the flavor of the hay smoke, flipping the steaks at least once, as you continue to grill another 15 to 20 minutes, until steaks are medium or medium rare.

Sprinkle with olive oil, salt, and pepper, and garnish with lemon wedges. Try some lemon juice on a bite to see if you like it.

Serve with chilled mountain spring water, Chianti, and Tuscan white beans on the side. The beans are essential, because Tuscans are nicknamed "bean eaters" throughout Italy.

Bread salad is also a good side dish.

Note: Be careful! Hay ignites quickly. Wear your welder's gloves when putting the hay on the fire.

ST. PATRICK'S IRISH BARBECUE STEW

SERVES 4 TO 6

This recipe was inspired by the life of St. Patrick. He first lived in Ireland as a slave who tended cattle. On his journey of escape from slavery, he and the sailors he traveled with were near starvation when a herd of pigs crossed their path. Barbecued pig saved the day and the saint.

You can barbecue the meat for this recipe a day ahead and refrigerate, or buy the meat from a local barbecue restaurant, or use leftover barbecue from your freezer. If you are cooking the meat for this recipe, get an 8-pound pork shoulder and a 10-pound untrimmed brisket. Barbecue the shoulder for 9 hours at 275°, and the brisket for 12 hours at 275°. Use 5 cups of water-soaked pecan or Jack Daniel's barrel chips for smoke.

1 large sweet yellow onion, chopped
4 medium unpeeled red potatoes, chopped
5 carrots, peeled and chopped
2 leeks, white ends only, cut into $\frac{1}{4}$-inch slices
5 tablespoons unsalted butter
1 pound barbecue beef brisket or rump roast, cubed
1 pound barbecued Boston butt (pork shoulder), cubed
Salt and pepper to taste
Pinch of powdered African bird pepper or cayenne
    pepper (optional)
$\frac{1}{2}$ pint Guinness Extra Stout
1 jigger Old Bushmills Irish Whiskey
1 cup water
1 cup Brook's House of Bar-B-Q Original
    Barbecue Sauce

Sauté the vegetables in butter until slightly tender, about 20 minutes. Add the whiskey and stout and allow the vegetables to simmer another 5 minutes. Put the meat, vegetables, and juices in a ceramic casserole. Pour barbecue sauce on top, followed by the water. Bake uncovered at 300° for 1 hour.

Serve the stew in individual ceramic bowls or in green cabbage bowls on a plate, with fresh Irish soda bread or sourdough bread, Blarney cheese, and Lazy Leprechaun Pickled Red Cabbage.

LAZY LEPRECHAUN PICKLED RED CABBAGE

SERVES 4 TO 6

This recipe is so named because it is a shortcut to the traditional boiled, multiple-day process.

1 small red cabbage, shredded
1 tablespoon sea salt
2 tablespoons sugar
2 cups white distilled vinegar

Put the shredded cabbage in a glass bowl. Sprinkle salt and sugar on top. Add the vinegar. Cover and refrigerate overnight, or 8 hours. Toss after 8 hours. Keep the cabbage in the refrigerator until you're ready to serve it, or serve it at room temperature.

DIXIE POTATO SLAW

SERVES 4 TO 6

This recipe combines two Southern favorites, coleslaw and potato salad, into one fantastic side dish.

1/4 cup Big Bob Gibson BBQ White Sauce, Cottonfields BBQ Sauce, or Bubba Brand White Sauce
1 tablespoon Shealy's BBQ Sauce, Maurice's BBQ Sauce, Johnny Harris BBQ Sauce, Rumboggie's BBQ Sauce, or Ella's Ultimate BBQ Sauce
1 teaspoon kosher or sea salt
1/4 teaspoon freshly ground black pepper
2 cups shredded cabbage or prepared coleslaw mix
4 or 5 medium-sized red, unpeeled potatoes
1/4 cup roasted or grilled red bell peppers, chopped
1/4 cup chopped red onion

Boil the potatoes in a covered pan for 45 minutes until tender. Drain the water from the pan, let the potatoes cool, pull the jackets off, discard the jackets, and cut the potatoes into small cubes.

Small jars of roasted red peppers are available in the pickle or Italian foods section of most supermarkets. To grill red bell peppers, cut the pepper in half lengthwise and remove the seeds and pulp. Grill the peppers over hot charcoal, turning frequently with tongs, until tender and charred.

Stir together the barbecue sauces, salt, and pepper. Combine all the ingredients in a bowl and gently toss. Chill for an hour or more.

PIG CIGARS

These edible "cigars" are best as appetizers or hors d'oeuvres. Egg-roll wrappers differentiate pig cigars from burritos, though the idea clearly owes homage to Mexican cuisine. Pig cigars are also reminiscent of Chinese spring rolls.

Each recipe below includes chopped barbecued pork shoulder, which you can prepare at home or buy from a barbecue restaurant.

The basic technique for preparing a cigar is to put an egg-roll wrapper on a plate and brush the wrapper with melted butter. Place a small portion of meat—about 1/4 cup—and other ingredients, if indicated, on the wrapper and roll the cigar. Brush the outside of the cigar with melted butter. Shape the ends in the style of a cigar.

Place the cigars on a greased cookie sheet and bake in a preheated oven at 325° for 20 minutes.

WANGO TANGO PIG TORPEDO

SERVES 4 (2 APPETIZER CIGARS PER PERSON)

This is a cigar for fiery eaters who like to dance.

8 egg-roll wrappers
$1/4$ pound unsalted butter, melted
2 cups barbecued pork, chopped
1 Fuji apple, chopped, and marinated in the juice of 1 lime for 5 minutes
1 cup Dinosaur Wango Tango Barbecue Sauce

Place one egg-roll wrapper on a plate and brush the exposed side of the wrapper with melted butter. Place $1/4$ cup chopped barbecued pork in a row, lengthwise, near the edge of the egg-roll wrapper. Roll the wrapper in the shape of a cigar. Brush the outside of the cigar with melted butter. Repeat this procedure 7 times.

Place the cigars on a cookie sheet and bake in a preheated oven at 325° for 20 minutes, until golden brown.

Serve on a black plate. Garnish with chopped Fuji apple. Use a plastic squeeze bottle filled with 1 cup Dinosaur Wango Tango Barbecue sauce to paint a zig zag pattern across the torpedoes.

CONGRESSIONAL PORK ROBUSTO MADURO

SERVES 4 (2 APPETIZER CIGARS PER PERSON)

This recipe is ideal for the 2nd Tuesday of November and the 4th of July.

8 egg-roll wrappers
$\frac{1}{4}$ pound unsalted butter, melted
2 cups barbecued pork, chopped
$\frac{1}{4}$ teaspoon powdered cayenne pepper
$\frac{1}{2}$ cup crumbled fried pork rinds
$\frac{1}{4}$ cup white onions, minced
$\frac{1}{4}$ cup red bell pepper, chopped
1 cup blue corn tortilla chips, crumbled
1 cup bright red tomato-based barbecue sauce

Place one egg-roll wrapper on a plate and brush the exposed side of the wrapper with melted butter. Place $\frac{1}{4}$ cup chopped barbecued pork in a row, lengthwise, near the edge of the egg-roll wrapper. Sprinkle the meat with cayenne pepper and 2 pinches of crumbled pork rinds. Roll the wrapper in the shape of a cigar. Brush the outside of the cigar with melted butter. Repeat this procedure 7 times.

Place the cigars on a cookie sheet and bake in a preheated oven at 325° for 20 minutes, until golden brown.

Serve on a white plate. Garnish with chopped onion and red bell pepper. Use a plastic squeeze bottle filled with 1 cup bright red tomato-based barbecue sauce to paint a striped pattern across the cigars. Circle the edge of the plate with crumbled blue corn tortilla chips.

REDNECK MOTHER
PANATELA COLORADO

SERVES 4 (2 APPETIZER CIGARS PER PERSON)

This recipe was inspired by Jerry Jeff Walker's rendition of the song "Up Against the Wall, Redneck Mother."

8 egg-roll wrappers
$\frac{1}{4}$ pound unsalted butter, melted
2 cups barbecued pork, chopped
$\frac{1}{4}$ teaspoon powdered cayenne pepper
8 tablespoons Sonny Bryan's Mild Barbecue Sauce
1 fresh red tomato, chopped
$\frac{1}{3}$ cup tender cactus strips (available in the Mexican
    section of supermarkets; also called "nopalitos")

Place one egg-roll wrapper on a plate and brush the exposed side of the wrapper with melted butter. Place $\frac{1}{4}$ cup chopped barbecued pork in a row, lengthwise, near the edge of the eggroll wrapper. Roll the wrapper in the shape of a cigar. Brush the outside of the cigar with melted butter. Repeat this procedure 7 times.

Place the cigars on a cookie sheet and bake in a preheated oven at 325° for 20 minutes, until golden brown.

Serve on a glazed terra cotta plate. Spread 1 tablespoon of barbecue sauce on each cigar. Garnish with chopped red tomato and cactus strips.

RUMBOGGIES PIG AND
NOODLE SOUP

SERVES 4

This soup is especially good on a snappy fall day or a cold winter night.

1 batch Grandma Ham's noodles, or a 14-ounce
    package of frozen egg noodles
6 cups chicken broth
2 cups cubed barbecue pork shoulder or barbecue pork
    rib meat

¹/₃ cup Rumboggies Bar-B-Que Sauce
Salt and pepper to taste

Put the noodles in boiling chicken broth. Reduce the heat and simmer the noodles for 15 minutes. Add meat, barbecue sauce, and water, if needed. Simmer 5 more minutes. Season with more sauce; salt and pepper to taste.

GRANDMA HAM'S NOODLES

SERVES 4

I don't know if these noodles had anything to do with her longevity, but my great grandmother, Sarah Viola Ham, lived a hundred years, when it was more unusual than today to do so. One of her sons, my grandfather, "Daddy Bert" Hamm, insisted on adding another "m" to the Ham family name. This probably had nothing to do with his shorter life span, but I've always wondered.

1 egg
¹/₄ cup cream
1 cup flour
1 teaspoon salt

Put the ingredients in a bowl. Stir with a wooden spoon until ingredients are the consistency of bread dough. Roll out on floured board. Use a table knife to cut noodles in ¹/₄-inch wide strips. Let dry, uncovered, out in the open, an hour or so at room temperature. The noodles can be set aside in a plastic bag in the refrigerator for a week, or frozen in a plastic bag for up to 2 months.

DICKSON TENNESSEE GRIST MILL CORNBREAD

SERVES 4

This recipe was adapted from the original given to me when I bought some Dickson Grist Mill cornmeal in Lynchburg, Tennessee, at the Jack Daniel's world championship barbecue cooking contest several years ago.

For variations, add ¹/₃ cup drained canned corn or some chopped peppers, hot or mild, or both.

2 cups stone-ground cornmeal

2 cups buttermilk

2 eggs

1 teaspoon sugar

½ teaspoon salt

½ teaspoon baking soda

½ teaspoon baking powder

4 teaspoons melted butter

Stir together the ingredients until there are no dry spots of cornmeal or baking powder and place the dough in a greased 9-inch Pyrex pan or a greased #7 cast-iron skillet.

Preheat the oven to 450°. Bake for 20 minutes, or until crust is golden brown.

It's unlikely you'll have leftovers, but if so, keep the remaining corn bread in the refrigerator for up to 1 week.

RICH DAVIS'S KC MASTERPIECE BBQ SAUSAGE BALLS

SERVES 4

My friend Dr. Rich Davis gave me permission to share this with you. A variation of it appears in the instant barbecue classic *All About Bar-B-Q Kansas City–Style*, by Rich Davis and Shifra Stein (Kansas City: Pig Out Publications, 1995).

1 pound bulk seasoned turkey sausage

1 egg, beaten

⅓ cup bread crumbs

1 teaspoon rubbed sage

½ cup KC Masterpiece Hickory Flavor BBQ Sauce

2 tablespoons brown sugar

2 tablespoons white vinegar

1 tablespoon soy sauce

In a large bowl, combine the sausage, egg, bread crumbs, and sage. Shape the mixture into bite-sized balls. Brown the balls in an ungreased heavy skillet over high heat. Drain off the excess fat.

Mix together the barbecue sauce, brown sugar, vinegar, and soy sauce and add to the skillet.

Simmer over low heat for 20 minutes, stirring occasionally to prevent sticking.

Serve the meatballs hot, with toothpicks.

WILMA'S SEDONA BBQ DIP

SERVES 6

Wilma Garrabrant settled in the red rock high desert country of Arizona by way of New York City and Los Angeles over thirty years ago. She first settled amidst the remote ruins of a former Native American community in rural Sedona, halfway between Phoenix and the Grand Canyon. Today, to the fortunate pilgrims who have enjoyed the pleasures of her table, Wilma is one of the most celebrated chefs of Sedona.

I ate Wilma's Hot Beef Dip as an evening appetizer while a guest at Casa Sedona bed and breakfast. The next morning, after enjoying Wilma's superb Sonoran Poached Egg with Ancho Hollandaise on Polenta, I visited with Wilma and got her permission to adapt her recipe for this book. The recipe is an ideal use for leftover barbecue meats.

1 pound chopped barbecue brisket, pork rib meat, pork shoulder or chicken
$\frac{1}{2}$ cup chopped onion
1 clove garlic, minced
$1\frac{1}{4}$ cups tomato-based barbecue sauce
1 4-ounce can chopped green chiles
1 8-ounce package cream cheese, softened
$\frac{1}{3}$ cup grated pecorino, Monterey Jack, or Parmesan cheese

Combine all ingredients and bake at 325° in a ceramic chafing or baking dish about 20 minutes until heated through.

Serve with Navajo Fry Bread, cut into triangles for dipping or spreading. Pita bread or baguette slices may be substituted.

Note: Any Arizona sauce in this book is appropriate for this recipe (see index), or experiment with your favorite sauces. You can make a good homemade sauce by combining 8 ounces of tomato sauce, $\frac{1}{4}$ cup ketchup, $\frac{3}{4}$ teaspoon dried oregano, and 1 teaspoon sugar.

CAROLINA PAELLA

SERVES 4 TO 6

My "Arkansas Trav'ler" barbecue buddy, Jim Quessenberry, says the recipe for the fantastic sauce he makes came to him in a dream. I was awake when I got the idea for this, but the moment of inspiration felt like a dream. The result turned out to be far from a nightmare.

2 cups long grain white enriched rice
2 cups barbecued pork rib meat scraps, trimmed of
bone, fat, and gristle
2 grilled or baked andouille sausages (about 1 cup)
6 medium grilled or boiled shrimp (optional)
$\frac{1}{2}$ grilled or baked boneless/skinless chicken breast
1 medium Vidalia onion or other sweet onion
1 large collard leaf, chopped
$\frac{1}{3}$ cup chopped roasted red bell pepper (see page 134–135)
1 4-ounce can chopped green chiles
$\frac{1}{3}$ cup Shealy's Bar-B-Que Sauce or Maurice's
Carolina Gold
1 teaspoon sea salt or kosher salt

Cook the rice a day ahead and refrigerate it overnight.

In a large bowl, combine all of the ingredients. Put the ingredients in a baking dish and heat it in a preheated oven at 250° for 30 minutes until food is thoroughly heated. Serve immediately.

THINK DIFFERENT FIERY
WONTON TOSTADAS

SERVES 6

An Apple computer ad featuring a smiling Dalai Lama and the words "Think Different" inspired this appetizer recipe.

12 wonton wrappers
$\frac{1}{2}$ cup corn oil or peanut oil
I pound chopped barbecued pork shoulder, grilled boneless/skinless chicken breast, or barbecued tofu (use applewood smoke with all three)
$\frac{1}{2}$ cup chopped cabbage or packaged coleslaw cabbage
I tablespoon hoisin sauce
$\frac{1}{4}$ cup Khatsa Barbecue Sauce
I tablespoon Khatsa Tibetan Hot Sauce, Inner Beauty, Jump into an Open Grave, or Dinosaur Wango Tango

Heat the oil in a fry pan until it begins to smoke, then reduce heat to medium and fry wonton wrappers 3 or 4 at a time in oil, until crispy and golden. Remove cooked wonton wrappers with tongs.

Combine the remaining ingredients and spoon them onto the wonton wrappers.

Serve immediately, with forks or chopsticks.

Note: Vary amount of the sauces to suit your taste.

EASY BBQ CHILI

SERVES 4

Chili is no longer limited to winter, as barbecue is no longer limited to summer. This chili is easy and flavorful in any season.

I pound barbecued beef brisket, cubed
2 16-ounce cans pinto beans, rinsed and drained
I medium chopped yellow or white onion, sautéed in bacon grease
I roasted or sautéed red bell pepper, chopped (see page 134–135)

2 cups Head Country Bar-B-Q Sauce
1 cup water
1 tablespoon paprika
1 tablespoon powdered mustard
1 teaspoon powdered oregano
1 teaspoon powdered coriander

Combine all of the ingredients in a pan. Bring to a boil and reduce to simmer. Simmer, uncovered, for 30 minutes. Taste, and adjust the spices and sauce to your liking.

Variation: Serve the chili Cincinnati style. Cook some bow tie, penne, macaroni, shell, or other pasta. Put the pasta in a chili bowl and cover it with chili. Sprinkle a small amount of powdered cinnamon and grated nutmeg on top. You can also add shredded Cheddar cheese and chopped fresh onions.

UNCLE CHUCK'S BBQ BALONEY SANDWICH

MAKES 1 SANDWICH

Barbecued baloney is an Oklahoma favorite. It is also appreciated in Texas, often in the form of smaller, baloney or sausage, spicy hot links.

My uncle Chuck Rains was an independent cement contractor for many years in Oklahoma City. Most of his business was putting in floors, driveways, and sidewalks for new houses. When I worked for him several summers, I grew to love a plain baloney sandwich with onions and cold milk for lunch. It would have been even better as adapted below. Tastes best when sitting on red dirt in the shade of an elm tree on a hot, dry, summer day in Oklahoma.

1 thick slice of barbecued baloney
1 slice fresh sweet onion
1 tablespoon Head Country Bar-B-Q Sauce, Maurice's, or Shealy's mustard-based barbecue sauce
2 slices white sandwich bread

Put baloney, onion, and sauce between 2 slices of bread.

LOVE POTION ON THE SWINE SANDWICH

MAKES 1 SANDWICH

The Que Queens of Kansas City make the Love Potion. The ease of putting the sandwich together is inspired by the Pork Matrons Society of Memphis. The preparation of the sandwich may go beyond the limits of Pork Matrons's standards, however, since they don't believe in buttering toast. It's too much like cooking.

1 handful pulled barbecue pork (about 1½ cups)
1 tablespoon Love Potion for the Swine Barbecue Sauce
¼ cup coleslaw with vinegar dressing
1 hamburger bun

Put pork, sauce, and slaw in the bun and enjoy.

CHERRY VALLEY BARBECUE SPAGHETTI

SERVES 4

Although barbecue spaghetti is a famous Memphis original, I never knew about it until Jim Quessenberry told me about it. I've named this version after the birthplace of Jim's world champion Sauce Beautiful (temporarily out of production).

1 pound package of spaghetti
1 pound barbecued pork shoulder, chopped
½ cup tomato-based barbecue sauce, such as Corky's
2 cups tomato sauce

Combine the meat, barbecue sauce, and tomato sauce in a saucepan. Bring to a boil, then reduce to simmer. Simmer for 45 minutes, stirring occasionally with a wooden spoon.

Cook the spaghetti in boiling water until tender and firm, or as directed on the package. Drain, rinse in a colander with hot water, and serve with sauce.

Note: Try other sauces, and vary the amount of barbecue sauce, to discover which sauce gives you the best flavor.

BONE SUCKIN' BLOODY MARY

SERVES 1

1 cup tomato juice
1 shot of vodka
2 tablespoons Bone Suckin' Sauce
1 cup crushed or cubed ice
1 spear of fresh, steamed, crunch asparagus, or one
    fresh carrot stick, 8 inches long

Combine the ingredients in a tall glass.

Garnish with the asparagus or carrot, decorated with a poultry tu tu.

SWEET POTATO PIE

SERVES 6

When I eat barbecue, I rarely save room for dessert. If I do save room, my favorite dessert with a barbecue meal is the old Southern favorite, sweet potato pie.

2 cups baked sweet potatoes
$3/4$ cup light brown sugar
2 eggs, slightly beaten
2 cups whole milk
3 tablespoons melted sweet butter
1 teaspoon cinnamon
$3/4$ teaspoon powdered ginger
$1/2$ teaspoon powdered nutmeg
$3/4$ teaspoon salt
1 9-inch unbaked pie shell

Bake 3 large unpeeled sweet potatoes at 350° for 1 hour until tender. Cut each potato in half and scoop the potato flesh into a bowl.

Preheat oven to 425°.

Mix together the potatoes, sugar, eggs, milk, and butter. Add the spices. Mix again and pour the mixture into unbaked pie crust.

Bake for about 1 hour, until the pie is set and lightly browned.

GLOSSARY
BASIC BARBECUE AND SAUCE TALK

The following barbecue glossary is not comprehensive, but it will help you feel at home around the pit and the sauce pot.

Anchovies: Small, silvery fish from the Mediterranen Sea, often preserved in salt or brine. A frequently used flavor enhancer in barbecue sauce and other sauces.

Barbecue: A method of cooking food in a covered pit at a low temperature (180° to 250°) with hardwood or hardwood coals for several hours.

Bark: The crusty outside of a properly barbecued pork shoulder or butt; called "brown" when ordered in a pork sandwich. The crusty, flat end of barbecued brisket is called burnt ends.

Baste; basting sauce: Liquid seasonings that are applied to barbecue during the cooking process. May be applied with a floor mop, dish mop, or brush. Floor mops are used for large animals or large quantities of meat; dish mops or brushes are used for smaller portions. The best mop has an all-cotton head, with a wooden handle. The best brush is wooden-handled with boar bristles. Basting sauce contains little or no sugar, corn syrup, fructose, molasses, or other ingredients that may burn onto the meat during the cooking process. Bastes are also referred to as mopping or sopping sauces; some are used as marinades.

Binder: A substance that holds the ingredients of a sauce together; cornstarch, prepared mustard, and xanthan gum are common barbecue sauce binders.

Bodacious: An assertive flavor or a wild and spirited lifestyle.

Burnt ends: What Kansas Citians call the crusty meat from a barbecued beef brisket. "Burned ends" or "brisket bark" is not acceptable terminology. To order "burned ends" or "brisket bark" in Kansas City would at best provoke laughter or at worst leave you empty-handed and misunderstood.

Chopped pork: A method of serving pork shoulder or butt. The meat is sliced, or "pulled," then cleavered into small pieces for sandwiches.

Cold sauce: Mixed from prepared ingredients; not cooked.

Dipping sauce: In this book, a sauce that works best on the side, in a bowl or puddle; this gives you control over how much sauce you use with each bite. Dipping sauce may also be poured on your barbecue. Sauces used for for dipping or pouring are best heated or at room temperature.

Done barbecue: Some pitmasters start sipping from a full bottle of whiskey when the meat is put in the barbecue pit; the barbecue is done when the bottle is empty. A more technical standard is that it's done when the meat is fully cooked, tender, and the fat is rendered from the meat. Federal regulations specify that done barbecue should weigh no more than 70 percent of the original uncooked weight.

Finish: As used in this book, a sauce's finish is the last flavor to register on your palate.

Finishing sauce: A sauce that is brushed or mopped on foods during the last 15 to 20 minutes of cooking.

Grill sauce: A sauce that is brushed or mopped on foods before and during the grilling process; some are used as marinades or dipping sauces.

Grilling: A method of cooking food on a grid or skewer, directly over hot flames or coals. Grilled food is cooked fast, at high temperatures.

Ketchup: also called *catsup.* A condiment made of tomatoes, sugar, vinegar, and spices. Used as a base for many barbecue sauces. Ketchups were originally made with a variety of non-tomato foods, such as mushrooms or fruits.

Monosodium Glutamate (MSG): A tasteless sodium compound used widely as a flavor enhancer; may cause temporary reactions in the nervous system such as tightness of facial muscles, chest pressure, or numbness in people who are sensitive to it; an ingredient in many barbecue sauces. Ingredients such as "natural flavoring," "natural seasoning," and "hydrolized plant or vegetable protein" contain MSG.

Mop, mopping sauce: Liquid seasonings that are applied to barbecue during the cooking process; so called as reference to the tool used to apply the sauce—either a floor mop or dish mop. Mopping sauces are also referred to as basting sauces; some may also be used as marinades.

Pepper: An aromatic berry from the *Piper nigrum* plant. May be used fresh, pickled, or dried as a flavor enhancer in sauces. Ground black pepper is the most commonly used pepper in barbecue sauces.

Peppers: Fleshy, hollow fruit with seeds inside. Sizes vary from the size of a toenail to as large as a big fist, and flavors vary from sweet and mild to pungent and fiery. Sweet bell peppers, cayenne, seranno, jalapeño, chile, and habañero are the most widely used in barbecue sauces.

Pig pickin': Traditional Southern method of serving a whole hog that is cooked so tender that you can pick the meat from the bones; also refers to the event itself.

Pulled pork: A method of serving pork shoulder or butt. The meat is grabbed by the handful, usually for a sandwich. Since it pulls apart by the grain, pulled pork appears to be stringy.

Rub: A mixture of spices, herbs, and other seasonings or tenderizers applied to meat several hours before cooking. Most rubs are dry, with ingredients that have been ground to the consistency of coarse salt. Some rubs are wet pastes.

Scoville: An ingenious meaure of incremental fieriness in peppers invented in 1912 by pharmacologist Wilbur L. Scoville.

Skinned ribs: Pork ribs with the membrane removed from the bony side.

Table sauce: A pouring or dipping sauce that is placed on a dining table; usually served warm or at room temperature.

Tamarind: A tropical legume whose pulp is used in many barbecue sauces to add texture and flavor.

SOURCES
TOLL-FREE SAUCE

Here's a selection of toll-free numbers for barbecue or bar-becue sauce. This listing does not imply endorsement. You are responsible for the consequences of your choice to do business with any of these companies. May all of your consequences be pleasant ones.

Air Ribs: Barbecue from The County Line (800) AIR RIBS

All Cajun Food Co.
(800) 467-3613

Arizona Salsa Co.
(888) 996-7711

Ashman Manufacturing Co.
King Street Blues
(800) 641-9924

Aunt Bea's BBQ Sauce
(800) 241-1108

B-B-Q Buddies: Billy Bones, Bourbon Q, Suthpen's
(800) 222-8348

Bear Creek Smokehouse
(800) 950-BEAR

Best of the West: Bootlegger, Buckaroo, Cowgirl
(800) 972-1119

Boardroom Bar-B-Q
(800) 873-0710

Bob Sykes BarB-Q
(800) 44SYKES

Brazos Country Foods
(800) 8SAUCES

Butch's Bar-B-Q (KS)
(800) 466-4544

Cajun Grill
(800) 822-4766

Calido Chili Traders: Hot sauces and barbecue sauces
(800) 568-8468

Char-Broil: Sauces, cookers, tools
(800) 241-8981

Charlie Beigg's (888) 502-8595

Charlotte's Rib (800) 70SAUCE

Coach's Bar-B-Que
(888) COACH-08

Colony South Corporation: Bubba Brand BBQ Sauces
(800) 261-6410

Cookies Bar "B" "Q" Sauce
(800) 331-4995
(in IA: (800) 522-1968)

Cookshack Barbecue Sauce
(800) 423-0698

Couch's Original Sauce
(800) 264-7535

Country Gourmet
(800) 784-3472

Crazy Jerry (800) 347-2823

Dave's Gourmet (800) 758-0372

Desperado's BBQ & Rib Co. Sauces, rubs, mops, and more.
(800) 508-RIBS

Diamond Jim's (800) 462-1086

Dickey's Barbecue Pit
(800) 460-9000

Dixie Trail Farms
(800) 665-3869

Dot Jones Barbeque Sauce
(800) 357-2823

Dream Catchers Sauce Co.
(888) 231-5867

Exclusively Barbecue: Many many sauces (800) 948-1009

Flamingo Flats (800) 468-8841

Floribbean Tropical BBQ Sauce
(800) 282-8459

Ford's Foods, Inc.: Bone Suckin' Sauce (800) 446-0947

Fromary's Heart BBQ Sauces
(888) FROMARY

Garden Row Foods
(800) 555-9798

Gates Bar-B-Q (800) 662-RIBS

Geno's (800) 93-GENOS

Golden Whisk (800) 742-1717

Goldwater's (800) 488-4932

Gourmet Emporium and Cheese Shop (800) 291-9463

Great Barbecue Sauce Catalog: Big selection of sauces
(800) 672-8237

Great Food Online
(800) 841-5984

Great Southern Sauce Co.:Lots of sauce (800) 437-2823

Hawaiian Plantations
(800) 767-4650

Head Country (888) 762-1227

Hillsdale Bank Bar-B-Q Sauce
(913) 783-4333

Hot Stuff Spicy Foods
(800) WANT HOT

House of Fire (800) 717-5787

Inner Beauty: Gourmet America
(800) 352-1352

Jack's Old South Bar-B-Que Sauce (888) 554-JACK

Jakarta (800) 678-TFRI

Jake Edward's Bar-B-Que
(888) 449-0488

Jardine's 7J Ranch
(888) 544-0110

Jo B's (800) 496-7889

Johnny D's (800) BASTEIT

Johnny Harris (888) JHSAUCE

KC Masterpiece
(800) 53-SAUCE

Kings Oink Express
(800) 332-OINK

Last Roundup
(800) 838-7497

Legend Barbecue Sauces
(800) 621-5075

Lehmann Farms Big Jake's
(800) 446-5276

Lloyd's Barbeque Sauce
(800) 999-RIBS

Lollipop Tree
(800) 842-6691

Louisiana Catalog
(800) 375-4100

Lynchburg Barbecue Sauce
(800) YUMM911

Mad Dog (800) 61-SAUCE

Mannon's Spice Co.
(888) 244-7888

Maurice's Flying Pig
(800) MAURICE

McIlhenny Farms/Tabasco
(800) 634-9599

Mo Hotta Mo Betta
(800) 462-3220

Moonlite (800) 322-8989

Mrs. Dog (800) 2MRS DOG

Nodine's Smokehouse
(800) 222-2059

Oasis Foods (888) 509-1863

Oklahoma Joe's (800) 232-3398

Old Fort (800) 245-FORT

Original Habanero Co.
(800) 946-9401

Paul's Pantry (888) 488-4300

Penderey's Taste Merchants: Sauces, books, tools, and more
(800) 533-1870

Pepper Creek Farms
(800) 526-8132

Peppers: BBQ sauces, hot sauces & more (800) 998-3473

Pigman's (800) 442-5207

Pig Out Publications: BBQ books and Love Potion for the Swine (800) 877-3119

Piquant Pepper (800) 931-7474

Puddle Jumpers: Acid Rain, Whisky Basin, and more
(800) 490-7602

Rendezvous (888) HOGS FLY

Robert Rothschild: Stockyard
BBQ Sauce (800) 356-8933

Rowena's (800) 627-8699

Saguaro: Cool Coyote
(800) 732-2447

Salsas Etc!: Salsas, hot sauces,
barbecue sauces, rubs, and more
(800) 407-2572

Santa Fire (888) 6TOMATO

Sauce Emporium
(888) 728-2371

Specialty Sauces: Excellent selection of BBQ sauces
(800) SAUCES-1

Spicy Jones
(800) 200-3559 (Texas only)

Stache Foods: Blackburn's Maple
BBQ Sauce (800) 255-8401

Stonewall Kitchen (800) 207-5267

Texas Stampede (800) 946-9401

Tombstone Prospecting Co.
(888) WYATT EARP

Tortuga Rum Co.
(800) 444-0625

Twin Peaks: Hot sauces and
barbecue sauces you'll want.
(888) 487-3257

Two Buddies (800) 48-SAUCE

Two Plates Full (800) 443-1711

Van's Pig Stand (800) 319-7624

Walker's Wood Jamaican Jerk
(800) 827-0769

W. B. Williams (888) 323-2324

Wicker's (800) 847-0032

Willingham's (800) 737-WHAM

Wireless (800) 669-9999

Yamaka (800) 560-3613

BURIAL SAUCE NOTE: Due to
popular demand, here's how to
get Jump into an Open Grave
BBQ Sauce directly from the
source. If can't find it locally or
through some of the toll-free or
Internet vendors, call Big Daddy
or Big Mama Gelinas at Big
Daddy's General Store, 516-541-
0144. You may as well get a case,
because you're likely to keep emp-
tying the precious stuff on your
ribs before the Grim Reaper finds
you. Store a bottle in your safety
deposit box to assure that it's there
when you need it.

SAUCE ON THE WEB

New Web sites are born daily. Here's a selection I picked up while
doing research for this book. Change is the one constant in
inner space, outer space, and cyberspace, so some of these
addresses may have changed or disappeared. No endorsement is
implied. You are strictly responsible for the consequences of
choosing to do business with any of the vendors listed. I hope all
of your consequences are pleasant.

Air Ribs: www.airribs.com

American Spoon Foods:
www.spoon.com

Annie Chun's:
www.anniechun.com

Armadillo Willy's:
www.armadillowillys.com

Big Rick's:
www.feist.com/~bigrick

Bob Sykes BarB-Q:
www.bobsykes.com

Boomer's Heroes BBQ Sauce:
www.boomersbbq.com

Butch's BBQ (NJ):
www.smackyourlipsbbq.com

Cajun Grill: www.Cajungrill.com

Charlie Beigg's:
www.charliebeiggs.com

Charlie Robinson's:
www.robinsbbqsauce.com

Claude's: www.claudessauces.com

Coach's Bar-B-Que:
www.coachsbbq.com

Cookies Bar "B" "Q" Sauce:
www.cookiesbbq.com

Cookshack: www.cookshack.com

Cotton Fields:
www.suncompsvc.com/cottonfields

Dave's Gourmet:
www.davesgourmet.com

David's Real Pit BBQ:
www.lavapit.com

Desperado's BBQ & Rib Co.:
www.lickmyribs.com

Dickey's Barbecue:
www.dickeys.com

Dixie Trail Farms:
www.dixietrail.com

El Paso Chile Company:
www.elpasochile.com

Famous Dave's:
www.famousdaves.com

Fromary's Heart Gourmet BBQ:
www.members.aol.com

Geno's: www.genossauce.com

Golden Whisk:
www.goldenwhisk.com

Goldwater's:
www.greatfood.com/goldwaters

Gourmet Emporium:
www.sendagift.websbest.com

Great Food: www.greatfood.com

Great Southern Sauce Co.:
www.greatsauce.com

Ham I Am!:
www.greatfood.com/hamiam

Harry and David:
www.harry-david.com

Hat's True Texas BBQ Sauce:
www.hatsbbq.com

Hawg Pen: www.hawgpen.com

Hoosier Sauce Co.:
www.hoosierhotsauce.com

Jack's Old South:
www.jacksoldsouth.com

Jardine's 7J Ranch:
www.jardinefoods.com

Jer-n-Al's BBQ Sauce:
www.jer-n-als.com

Kansas Barbecue Sauces:
www.kansascommerce.com

KC Masterpiece:
www.kingsford.com

Khatsa: www.khatsa.com

Kings: www.kingsbbq.com

Land of Odds:
www.landofodds.com

Lynchburg Barbecue Sauce:
www.boarsbreath.com

Mad Pepper Co.:
www.market21.com/madpepco

Oklahoma Agriculture Dept.:
www.oklaosf.state.ok.us-okag

Oklahoma Joe's:
www.rbjb.com/rbjb/oklahoma/joes.htm

Pigman: www.pigman.com

Salsa Express:
www.salsaexpress.com

Sam McGees:
www.sammcgees.com

Seasoning To Service:
www.seasoning.com

Smoke Ring [bbq links]:
www.smokering.com

Smokestack Lightning:
www.pitbossbbq.com

Tombstone Prospecting Co.:
www.tombstone1877.com

Twin Peaks Gourmet Trading Post: www.tpeaks.com

Uncle Dougie's:
www.user.mc.net/~udougies

USA Smoke: www.usa-smoke.com

Willingham's:
www.willinghams.com

Wing-Time: www.wingtime.com

Yamaka: www.interpac.net/~rfc

BOOKS ABOUT SAUCE AND BARBECUE

Some of my favorite books on sauce, barbecue sauce, and barbecue are listed below. This is a good place to start if the subject is new to you.

SAUCE

The Saucier's Apprentice, by Raymond Sokolov (NY: Alfred A. Knopf, 1992) Sauce history, basics, and recipes. No discussion of barbecue, but Mr. Sokolov includes a bearnaise sauce recipe which he calls the "preeminent sauce" for grilled meat.

The Sauce Bible—Guide to the Saucier's Craft, by David Paul Larousse (NY: John Wiley & Sons, 1993) Light on barbecue sauce, but heavy on sauce history, basics, sauce recipes, food recipes, tools, and how to paint with sauce.

BARBECUE SAUCE

Paul Kirk's Championship Barbecue Sauces, by Paul Kirk (Boston: The Harvard Common Press, 1998) The baron of barbecue has prepared some of the best sauces, rubs, bastes, and barbecue I've ever tasted. This book is essential for anyone who is serious about making great barbecue sauce. Paul describes the basic barbecue method of cooking. He also tells where to get spices, meats, cookers, tools, barbecue videos, and cooking classes.

The Ultimate Barbecue Sauce Cookbook, by Jim Auchmutey and Susan Puckett (Marietta, GA: Longstreet Press, 1995) Jim and Susan introduce an international and regional variety of excellent barbecue sauce recipes. History, anecdotes, and sources are also included. Informative, entertaining, beautifully presented, and absolutely essential for barbecue sauce devotees and casual backyard pitmasters.

Salsas, Sambals, Chutneys & Chowchows, by Chris Schlesinger and John Willoughby (NY: William Morrow & Co., 1993) Easily prepared, fabulous recipes that you can make with fresh ingredients. Many will become your instant favorites. Color photos show how to artfully present most of the dishes.

The Great Barbecue Companion— Mops, Sops, Sauces, and Rubs, by Bruce Bjorkman (Freedom, CA: Crossing Press, 1996) Bruce "Mr. Barbecue" Bjorkman packs fun, insights, adventure, practical pit guidance, facts, anecdotes, and loads of great mop, sop, sauce, and rub recipes in this lively tribute to American barbecue.

BARBECUE

All About Bar-B-Q Kansas City-Style, by Rich Davis and Shifra Stein (Kansas City, MO: Pig Out Publications, 1995) Dr. Rich Davis is the creator of KC Masterpiece Barbecue Sauce. He and his sons, Rich Jr. and Charley, originated the immensely popular KC Masterpiece Barbecue & Grill in Kansas City, St. Louis, and other cities. In this book, Dr. Davis and coauthor Shifra Stein share valuable tips on the barbecue method of cooking, plus excellent barbecue, sauce, side dish, and dessert recipes.

The Kansas City Barbecue Society Cookbook, by the members of the Society (Nashville, TN: Favorite Recipes Press) This book benefits from the collective strength of a talented group of cooks and pitmasters. The book includes methods, tools, tips, and recipes for competition or recreational cooks.

Jack Daniel's Old Time Barbecue Cookbook, by Vince Staten (Louisville, KY: The Sulgrave Press, 1991) Here the coauthor of the classic barbecue adventure book *Real Barbecue* introduces some of the best barbecue recipes that are legal to print. A bonus is Vince's inimitable style, humor, and some photos that will make your mouth water and your heart long to be a citizen of Moore County.

The New Texas Cuisine, by Stephan Pyles (NY: Doubleday, 1993) A priceless collection of recipes, history, techniques, tips, and humor from one of the world's most gifted chefs. Many of the recipes are a creative fusion of Southwestern and French cooking. Beautiful photographs, including some masterful examples of sauce painting.

The Thrill of the Grill, by Chris Schlesinger and John Willoughby (NY: William Morrow & Co., 1990) I have admired Chris Schlesinger's culinary talents since meeting him at Memphis In May more than a decade ago. This volume from Schlesinger and coauthor John Willoughby is already a classic. Recipes, techniques, history, anecdotes, and humor you mustn't miss.

Smoke & Spice, by Cheryl Alters Jamison and Bill Jamison (Boston, MA: The Harvard Common Press, 1994) Cheryl and Bill have done their homework—on the road, at barbecue cooking contests, and home at the pit. This book is a treasury of barbecue techniques, recipes, and anecdotes. Includes some excellent barbecue sauce recipes.

Smokestack Lightning — Adventures in the Heart of Barbeque Country, by Lolis Eric Elie; photographs by Frank Stewart (NY: Farrar, Straus, and Giroux, 1996) Lolis and Frank toured the country, talked with many barbecuers, took pictures, and did a lot of eating and thinking. The result is a classic book on American barbecue history, sociology, and philosophy. It is spiced with social commentary, photo essays, cooking insights, and a superb selection of recipes. This book already stands among the giants of barbecue literature.

John Willingham's World Champion Bar-B-Q, by John Willingham (NY: William Morrow & Co., 1996) John has bragging rights as one of the most decorated championship pitmasters of all time. When he isn't winning contests, he makes Wham Cookers, Wham Sauces, Wham Rubs, and runs his barbecue restaurant in Memphis. Thanks to Will Schwalbe, editor-in-chief, William Morrow & Co., for persuading John to sit down long enough to write one of the best books in the genre.

If you can't find these books at your local or cyberspace bookseller, try Karen Adler's Pig Out Publications, world's largest "One Stop BBQ & Grill Bookshop." (800) 276-8525. Kansas Citians can call 531-3119. www.barbecuen.com/pigout

BARBECUE SAUCE EVENTS

Many sauce contests are held in conjunction with barbecue cooking contests. Entries are usually limited to the teams competing in the meat-cooking contest. With few exceptions, sauces are judged either with a spoon, or on a piece of bread, instead of on unseasoned barbecue meat.

Judging panels range from the general public to celebrities, chefs, and food critics. Judging formats range from a popular vote for known products to blind judging of unlabeled products on the basis of appearance, aroma, texture, flavor, or other qualities.

For information on hundreds of barbecue cooking contests, contact the Kansas City Barbeque Society, (800) 963-5227, or USA Smoke, www.usa-smoke.com

---

American Royal International Barbecue Sauce, Rub, and Baste Contest
Governor's Exposition Building, American Royal Complex
American Royal Association
1701 American Royal Court
Kansas City, MO 64102
(816) 221-9800
e-mail: amroyalbbq@aol.com
www.americanroyal.com

The contest is held the first Saturday of October, in conjunction with American Royal Barbecue. It began in 1984 as the Diddy-Wa-Diddy National Barbecue Sauce Contest. Now the world's largest, most prestigious barbecue sauce, rub, and baste contest. Open to commercially available products only. Sauces are blind-judged on the basis of appearance, aroma, flavor without meat, and flavor with real barbecued pork and beef. Rubs and bastes are blind-judged on the basis of product appearance and flavor, plus the flavor of barbecued pork ribs cooked with the product.

Battle of the Sauces
Raleigh, North Carolina
(919) 833-7647

This battle takes place in early March. The public samples local commercially available sauces. Each bottle purchased counts as one vote. It was started in 1992.

Fiery Foods Shows
The original Fiery Food Show was in 1988 in New Mexico. Since then, it has become enormously popular and has spawned other shows in other states. The emphasis is on hot sauces and other hot foods, but barbecue sauces have commanded an increasingly popular niche. Sauces are judged by a panel of experts. The emphasis is on flavor blends and overall palatability. Final results for the coveted and prestigious Scovie Awards, named after Wilbur Scovie, are announced at the show.

For information contact Sunbelt Shows, (505) 298-3835; fax (505) 298-3826, or e-mail: chile@fiery-foods.com Web site: www.fiery-foods.com
The Web site includes excellent links to products, manufacturers, and shops that sell sauce.

BARBECUE ORGANIZATIONS

There are three essentials to improving your barbecue:
(1) Read books and articles about barbecue cooking.
(2) Cook frequently and keep notes on what works and what doesn't.
(3) Join a barbecue organization and actively participate.
It's likely that one of the following organizations, or members of one of these organizations, is near your neighborhood.

Big Apple BBQ Association
c/o Richard Alexander
7 East 14th Street - Suite 919
New York, NY 10003
(212) 989-0021

California State Barbecue Association
c/o Frank Boyer
2911 Bear Creek Way
Los Gatos, CA 95030-9497
(408) 354-4693
www.cbbqa.com

Central Texas Barbecue Association
P.O. Box 4566
Temple, TX 76505
(254) 778-1756

East Texas Barbecue Cookers Association
2709 Cedarcrest
Marshall, TX 75670

Greater Houston Barbecue Society
www.angelfire.com/tx/GHBBQS

Greater Omaha Barbecue Society
4928 N. 105th
Omaha NE 68134
(402) 493-1474

Greater Wichita Barbeque Society
c/o Russ West
2135 N. Riverside Blvd.
Wichita, KS 67203
(316) 264-5115

International Barbecue Cookers Association
P.O. Box 300566
Arlington, TX 76007-0556
(817) 548-8894

Kansas City Barbeque Society
11514 Hickman Mills Drive
Kansas City, MO 64134
(800) 963-5227
www.barbeque.com

Lone Star Barbecue Society
c/o Pat Nicholas
P.O. Box 120771
Arlington, TX 76012-0771
(817) 261-9507
www.htcomp.net/bbq/lonestar

Memphis In May
245 Wagner Place - Suite 220
Memphis, TN 38103-3815
(901) 525-4611
memphisinmay.org

National Barbecue Association
P.O. Box 9685
Kansas City, MO 64134
(816) 767-8311
www.ribman.com/nbbqa

New England Barbecue Association
P.O. Box 97
North Billerica, MA 01862-0097
(978) 762-8504
www.netrelief.com/nebs

North Texas Barbecue Cookers Association
P.O. Box 3024
Denton, TX 76201
(817) 382-1942

Pacific Northwest Barbecue Association
c/o Bob Lyon
4244 134th Ave. S.E.
Bellevue, WA 98006
(206) 643-0607

Texas Gulf Coast Barbecue Cookers Association
26611 Weir Way
Magnolia, TX 77355
(281) 356-6244

West Texas Barbecue Association
P.O. Box 5615
Odessa, TX 79764
(915) 366-7227

Keep up with news from the barbecue community by subscribing to the following publications:

Goat Gap Gazette
P.O. Box 800
Brookesmith, Texas 76827
(915) 646-6914

National Barbecue News
P.O. Box 981
Douglas, Georgia 31533
(912) 384-9112

The Pitts
7714 Hillard
Dallas, Texas 75217
(214) 398-4374

The Griller's Backyard Barbecuer
14 Holbrook
Palmer, Massachusetts 01069

USA Smoke BBQ News
Rt. 2, Box 73-B
Hico, Texas 76457
(254) 785-2212
lola@usa-smoke.com

INDEX